# Easy
# Air Fryer
## Cookbook for Beginners  UK

*Makayla Lefroy*

## 2000+

Super Quick, Yummy and Affordable Recipes Book with Tips & Tricks to Air Fry, Grill, and Bake - UK Measurements & Ingredients

**Copyright© 2023 By Makayla Lefroy**

All rights reserved worldwide.

No part of this book may be reproduced or transmitted in any form or by any means, electronic or mechanical, including photo- copying, recording or by any information storage and retrieval system, without written permission from the publisher, except for the inclusion of brief quotations in a review.

**Warning-Disclaimer**

The purpose of this book is to educate and entertain. The author or publisher does not guarantee that anyone following the techniques, suggestions, tips, ideas, or strategies will become successful. The author and publisher shall have neither liability or responsibility to anyone with respect to any loss or damage caused, or alleged to be caused, directly or indirectly by the information contained in this book.

# Table of Contents

INTRODUCTION ................................................................... 1

Know about the Air Fryer ..................................................... 2

Pros and Cons of Air Fryer - To Fry or Not to Fry? ............... 3
Tips for Clean and Maintenance: ........................................ 6
Get Air Frying Today! ......................................................... 7

## Chapter 1   Breakfasts   8

Gluten-Free Granola Cereal ................................................ 9
Peppered Maple Bacon Knots ............................................. 9
Chimichanga Breakfast Burrito ........................................... 9
Southwestern Ham Egg Cups ............................................. 9
Egg Tarts ......................................................................... 10
Honey-Apricot Granola with Greek Yoghurt ...................... 10
Onion Omelette ............................................................... 10
Maple Granola ................................................................. 10
Spinach and Mushroom Mini Quiche ................................ 11
Breakfast Cobbler ............................................................ 11
Super Easy Bacon Cups ................................................... 11
Tomato and Mozzarella Bruschetta .................................. 11
Quick and Easy Blueberry Muffins ................................... 12
Egg White Cups ............................................................... 12
Canadian Bacon Muffin Sandwiches ................................ 12
Egg in a Hole ................................................................... 12
Butternut Squash and Ricotta Frittata ............................. 12
Spinach and Swiss Frittata with Mushrooms ................... 13
Berry Muffins .................................................................. 13
French Toast Sticks ......................................................... 13
Homemade Toaster Pastries ............................................ 13
Simple Scotch Eggs ......................................................... 14
Breakfast Sammies ......................................................... 14
Spinach Omelet ............................................................... 14
BLT Breakfast Wrap ......................................................... 14

## Chapter 2   Family Favorites   15

Scallops with Green Vegetables ....................................... 16
Puffed Egg Tarts .............................................................. 16
Cajun Shrimp ................................................................... 16
Steak and Vegetable Kebabs ........................................... 16
Pork Burgers with Red Cabbage Salad ............................ 17
Pecan Rolls ...................................................................... 17
Fried Green Tomatoes ..................................................... 17
Churro Bites .................................................................... 17
Mixed Berry Crumble ....................................................... 18
Meringue Cookies ............................................................ 18

## Chapter 3   Fast and Easy Everyday Favourites   19

Crunchy Fried Okra ......................................................... 20
Air Fried Butternut Squash with Chopped Hazelnuts ....... 20
Cheesy Chilli Toast .......................................................... 20
Air Fried Shishito Peppers ............................................... 20
Corn Fritters ................................................................... 21
Air Fried Broccoli ............................................................ 21
Buttery Sweet Potatoes .................................................. 21
Air Fried Tortilla Chips .................................................... 21
Simple and Easy Croutons .............................................. 21
Spinach and Carrot Balls ................................................. 21
Peppery Brown Rice Fritters ........................................... 22
Herb-Roasted Veggies ..................................................... 22

## Chapter 4  Poultry  23

- Chicken Schnitzel Dogs ................................. 24
- Easy Turkey Tenderloin ................................. 24
- Chicken Chimichangas .................................. 24
- Fried Chicken Breasts ................................... 25
- Sweet Chili Spiced Chicken ........................... 25
- Cranberry Curry Chicken ............................... 25
- Classic Whole Chicken .................................. 25
- Sweet and Spicy Turkey Meatballs ................ 26
- Chicken and Ham Meatballs with Dijon Sauce .................. 26
- Spanish Chicken and Mini Sweet Pepper Baguette ............. 26
- Fiesta Chicken Plate ...................................... 26
- Chicken Drumsticks with Barbecue-Honey Sauce ............. 27
- Hawaiian Huli Huli Chicken .......................... 27
- Bruschetta Chicken ....................................... 27
- Crispy Dill Chicken Strips ............................. 27
- Bacon-Wrapped Chicken Breasts Rolls ......... 28
- Wild Rice and Kale Stuffed Chicken Thighs ........ 28
- Easy Chicken Fingers .................................... 28
- Potato-Crusted Chicken ................................. 28
- Gochujang Chicken Wings ............................ 29
- Israeli Chicken Schnitzel ............................... 29
- Crispy Duck with Cherry Sauce ..................... 29
- Ham Chicken with Cheese ............................. 30
- Herb-Buttermilk Chicken Breast .................... 30
- Chicken Jalfrezi ............................................. 30

## Chapter 5  Vegetables and Sides  31

- Crispy Garlic Sliced Aubergine ...................... 32
- Polenta Casserole .......................................... 32
- Cauliflower Steaks Gratin .............................. 32
- Roasted Brussels Sprouts with Bacon ............ 32
- Cauliflower with Lime Juice .......................... 33
- Flatbread ........................................................ 33
- Indian Aubergine Bharta ................................ 33
- Mexican Corn in a Cup .................................. 33
- Cheese-Walnut Stuffed Mushrooms ............... 33
- Sweet-and-Sour Brussels Sprouts .................. 34
- Roasted Aubergine ........................................ 34
- Parmesan-Rosemary Radishes ....................... 34
- Breaded Green Tomatoes ............................... 34
- Tofu Bites ...................................................... 34
- Corn and Coriander Salad .............................. 35
- Mole-Braised Cauliflower .............................. 35
- Asparagus Fries ............................................. 35
- Brussels Sprouts with Pecans and Gorgonzola ......... 35
- Cabbage Wedges with Caraway Butter .......... 36
- Caesar Whole Cauliflower ............................. 36
- Marinara Pepperoni Mushroom Pizza ............ 36
- Broccoli with Sesame Dressing ..................... 36
- Sesame Carrots and Sugar Snap Peas ............ 37
- Easy Rosemary Green Beans ......................... 37
- Sweet and Crispy Roasted Pearl Onions ........ 37

## Chapter 6  Vegetarian Mains  38

- Cheesy Cauliflower Pizza Crust ..................... 39
- Roasted Vegetables with Rice ....................... 39
- Cayenne Tahini Kale ..................................... 39
- Stuffed Portobellos ........................................ 39
- Baked Turnip and Courgette .......................... 40
- Rice and Aubergine Bowl .............................. 40
- Loaded Cauliflower Steak ............................. 40
- Italian Baked Egg and Veggies ...................... 40
- White Cheddar and Mushroom Soufflés ........ 40
- Almond-Cauliflower Gnocchi ........................ 41

## Chapter 7  Beef, Pork, and Lamb  42

- Tomato and Bacon Zoodles ........................... 43
- German Rouladen-Style Steak ....................... 43
- Sausage and Pork Meatballs .......................... 43
- Cheese Crusted Chops ................................... 44
- Reuben Beef Rolls with Thousand Island Sauce ............. 44
- Sesame Beef Lettuce Tacos ........................... 44
- Mushroom in Bacon-Wrapped Filets Mignons ............. 44
- Goat Cheese-Stuffed Bavette Steak ............... 45
- Chicken-Fried Steak ...................................... 45
- Greek Pork with Tzatziki Sauce ..................... 45
- Panko Crusted Calf's Liver Strips .................. 45
- Italian Sausage Links .................................... 46

Bacon, Cheese and Pear Stuffed Pork ........................... 46
Pork Loin Roast ............................................................ 46
Blackened Steak Nuggets ............................................ 46
Mozzarella Stuffed Beef and Pork Meatballs ................. 47
Italian Pork Loin ........................................................... 47
Lamb and Cucumber Burgers ...................................... 47
Parmesan Herb Filet Mignon ........................................ 47
Parmesan-Crusted Steak .............................................. 48
Bacon-Wrapped Cheese Pork ...................................... 48
Peppercorn-Crusted Beef Fillet .................................... 48
Pork and Beef Egg Rolls .............................................. 48
Currywurst ................................................................... 49
Macadamia Nuts Crusted Pork Rack ............................ 49

## Chapter 8  Fish and Seafood                                    50

Roasted Halibut Steaks with Parsley ............................ 51
Cucumber and Salmon Salad ....................................... 51
Tuna Steak .................................................................. 51
Roasted Fish with Almond-Lemon Crumbs .................. 51
Coconut Prawns .......................................................... 52
Crunchy Air Fried Cod Fillets ....................................... 52
Trout Amandine with Lemon Butter Sauce ................... 52
Golden Prawns ............................................................ 52
Easy Scallops .............................................................. 53
Parmesan Mackerel with Coriander ............................. 53
Confetti Salmon Burgers .............................................. 53
Tex-Mex Salmon Bowl ................................................. 53
Baked Monkfish ........................................................... 53
Baked Salmon with Tomatoes and Olives .................... 54
Almond Catfish ............................................................ 54
Stuffed Sole Florentine ................................................ 54
Sesame-Crusted Tuna Steak ........................................ 54
Prawn Bake ................................................................. 54
Garlic Butter Prawns Scampi ....................................... 55
Fish Tacos with Jalapeño-Lime Sauce ......................... 55
Country Prawns ........................................................... 55
Almond-Crusted Fish ................................................... 55
Tuna-Stuffed Tomatoes ................................................ 56
Sea Bass with Potato Scales ....................................... 56
Sole and Cauliflower Fritters ........................................ 56

## Chapter 9  Snacks and Appetizers                               57

Crispy Green Bean Fries with Lemon-Yoghurt Sauce ........... 58
Greens Chips with Curried Yoghurt Sauce ................... 58
Easy Spiced Nuts ........................................................ 58
Spicy Chicken Bites .................................................... 58
Baked Spanakopita Dip ............................................... 59
Lebanese Muhammara ................................................ 59
Veggie Salmon Nachos ............................................... 59
Crispy Cajun Fresh Dill Pickle Chips ............................ 59
Italian Rice Balls ......................................................... 60
Parmesan Chips .......................................................... 60
Pepperoni Pizza Dip .................................................... 60
Roasted Grape Dip ...................................................... 60
Chilli-brined Fried Calamari ......................................... 61
Old Bay Chicken Wings ............................................... 61
Ranch Oyster Snack Crackers ..................................... 61
Prawns Toasts with Sesame Seeds ............................. 61
Taco-Spiced Chickpeas ............................................... 62
Crunchy Basil White Beans ......................................... 62
Stuffed Fried Mushrooms ............................................ 62
Root Veggie Chips with Herb Salt ................................ 62
Artichoke and Olive Pitta Flatbread .............................. 62
Poutine with Waffle Fries ............................................. 63
Classic Spring Rolls .................................................... 63
Mexican Potato Skins .................................................. 63
Beef and Mango Skewers ............................................ 64

## Chapter 10  Desserts                                          65

Crustless Peanut Butter Cheesecake ........................... 66
Brown Sugar Banana Bread ......................................... 66
Caramelized Fruit Skewers .......................................... 66
Dark Brownies ............................................................. 66
Indian Toast and Milk .................................................. 67
Apple Fries .................................................................. 67
Butter Flax Cookies ..................................................... 67
Pineapple Wontons ..................................................... 67
Grilled Pineapple Dessert ............................................ 68
Zucchini Bread ............................................................ 68
Lime Bars .................................................................... 68
Boston Cream Donut Holes ......................................... 68
Blueberry Cream Cheese Bread Pudding .................... 69
Lemon Poppy Seed Macaroons ................................... 69
Chocolate Soufflés ...................................................... 69

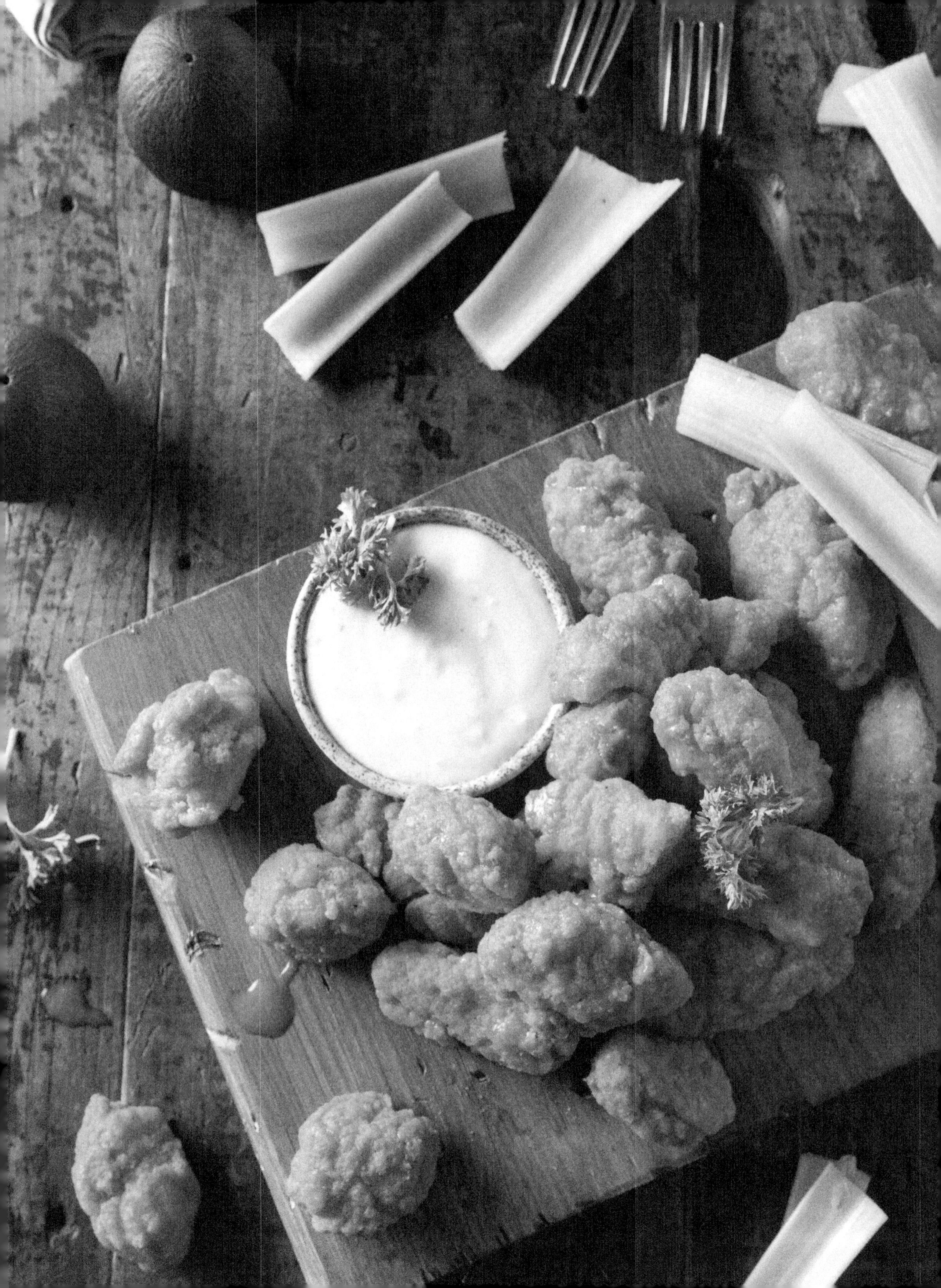

# INTRODUCTION

Do you love food but hate spending hours in the kitchen? We hear you! Life can be hectic, and finding the time to cook a nutritious meal can be a challenge. Enter the air fryer, your answer to quick and easy meals that taste like they've been cooked by a professional chef. This kitchen gadget is a must-have helper for foodies who want to enjoy delicious meals without the hassle. With the air fryer, you can cook everything from chicken wings to veggies in a fraction of the time, leaving you with more time to savor your creation.

Is that magic attracts you? If so, join me on the journey of air frying cooking! In this cookbook, I will guide you through the basic knowledge of the air fryer, its pros and cons, and all kinds of tips that could help you in the kitchen. I believe my sharing would definitely be very helpful for you, whether you're an air-frying expert or a beginner. So follow me, let's get started!

# Air Fryer: The Sizzling Technology

## Know about the Air Fryer

The Air Fryer is the new buzzword in the culinary world. It is a revolutionary machine that has taken the cooking world by storm. It works by utilizing the latest technology to circulate hot air around the food, resulting in crispy and golden-brown fried dishes with up to 80% less oil than traditional deep-frying methods. This unique mechanism ensures that the food is cooked evenly from all sides, and there is no need for constant stirring or flipping.

Not only does the Air Fryer cook food to perfection, but it also saves time and effort in the kitchen. You can now enjoy your favorite fried dishes without the hassle of preheating the oven or waiting for the oil to heat up. The Air Fryer is also equipped with a timer and temperature control, allowing you to customize the cooking process according to your preference.

But wait, there's more! The Air Fryer is not just limited to frying foods. You can use it to bake, roast, grill, and even reheat food. It's a versatile kitchen gadget that can replace several other appliances in your kitchen, saving you valuable counter space and money.

Don't just take my word for it. According to a study conducted by NPD Group, air fryer sales in the United States increased by 82% in 2019, with over 10 million units sold. This statistic proves that the Air Fryer is not just a passing fad, but a kitchen gadget that has become an essential part of many households.

In conclusion, the Air Fryer is a sizzling technology that has taken the culinary world by storm. It is a versatile, healthy, and time-saving kitchen gadget that can help you enjoy your favorite fried dishes guilt-free.

## Pros and Cons of Air Fryer - To Fry or Not to Fry?

As with any kitchen gadget, the Air Fryer has its fair share of pros and cons. It is important to weigh these factors before deciding whether to invest in one.

Pros:

1.Faster Cooking: The Air Fryer is equipped with a high-powered fan that circulates hot air around the food. This results in faster cooking times, allowing you to enjoy your meals in less time.

2.Versatility: The Air Fryer can do more than just fry. It can also bake, roast, grill, and reheat food. This makes it a versatile kitchen gadget that can replace several other appliances in your kitchen.

3.No Odors: Traditional deep frying can leave a lingering odor in your kitchen, but with the Air Fryer, you can avoid this problem. The device uses hot air instead of oil to cook, which means no lingering smells.

4.Less Fat: The Air Fryer is an ideal cooking solution for people who want to eat healthier. It uses less oil, which means fewer calories and less fat in your food.

5.Easy to Use: The Air Fryer is very easy to use, with a simple interface and straightforward instructions. You don't need to be an expert in cooking to get great results.

6.More Nutritious Food: The Air Fryer is a great way to cook vegetables, meats, and other foods while retaining their nutrients. This is because the hot air cooks the food quickly, which helps to preserve its nutritional value.

7.Less Mess: The Air Fryer eliminates the need for messy oil splatters, reducing clean-up time and effort.

8.Consistent Results: With the Air Fryer, you can achieve consistent results every time. This is because the device uses a precise temperature control system that ensures the food is cooked evenly.

Cons:

1.Limited Capacity: Air Fryers are typically small in size and can only cook small to medium-sized portions of food. This can be a disadvantage if you are cooking for a large family or hosting a party.

2.Size: While Air Fryers are relatively small, they still take up counter space in your kitchen. If you have a small kitchen, this may be a concern.

3.Cost: Air Fryers can be expensive, especially if you opt for a high-end model. This may not be a suitable investment for people on a budget.

4.Limited Food Options: Not all types of food can be cooked in an Air Fryer. Foods that are battered or have a wet coating may not turn out as crispy as you would like. This can be a disadvantage for people who love fried food but want a healthier option.

5.Requires Maintenance: The Air Fryer requires regular cleaning and maintenance to ensure it functions correctly.

6.Noise: The fan in the Air Fryer can be quite noisy, which may be a concern for some users.

Tips for Perfect Air Frying

Now that you know the basics of the Air Fryer, let's dive into some tips for perfect cooking with this fantastic kitchen gadget.

Essential Tips to Use:

1.Preheat the Air Fryer: Give your air fryer a head start by preheating it for a few minutes before cooking. Think of it like a warm-up before a workout - it'll help your food cook evenly and get that crispy exterior you crave.

2.Don't Overcrowd the Basket: It's tempting to pack your air fryer basket to the brim, but resist the urge! Overcrowding can cause your food to cook unevenly and stick together like clingy exes.

3.Use a Little Oil: Air frying uses less oil than traditional deep frying, but don't skimp entirely! A little oil goes a long way in making your food crispy and delicious. It's like a tiny flavor hug for your food.

4.Shake the Basket: Give your food a little shake, shake, shake to ensure it's cooking evenly and not sticking together like a group of middle school girls.

Special Tips to Cook Delicious:

1.Experiment with Different Spices and Seasonings: Don't be afraid to spice things up in the kitchen! Try different herbs and spices to add some pizzazz to your dishes. You might just discover a new favorite flavor combo.

2.Try Coating Your Food: Give your food a crunchy coat of armor with breadcrumbs, flour, or crushed nuts. It's like a delicious suit of armor protecting your food from the heat.

3.Cook at High Temperatures: Crank up the heat and get ready for some crispy goodness! Just be sure to keep an eye on your food so it doesn't go from golden brown to charcoal black.

4.Don't Be Afraid to Flip: It's not just for pancakes! Flipping your food halfway through the cooking process can help ensure it cooks evenly on both sides. Think of it like giving your food a little somersault - it'll appreciate the attention.

## Tips for Clean and Maintenance:

1.Clean Your Air Fryer After Each Use: Ain't nobody got time for a dirty air fryer! Clean the basket, drawer, and removable parts after each use to keep your air fryer in tip-top shape.

2.Use Non-Abrasive Cleaners: Abrasives are for exfoliating, not cleaning your air fryer. Stick to gentle cleaners to avoid damaging the non-stick coating.

3.Don't Overload the Basket: You're not playing Tetris with your food! Overloading the basket can cause a mess and make cleaning up a nightmare. Keep it simple and cook in batches if needed.

4.Check the Filter Regularly: Your air fryer's filter is like its lungs - it needs to breathe! Check and clean or replace the filter regularly to keep your air fryer happy and healthy.

## Get Air Frying Today!

Well, there you have it folks! With the essential knowledge about air fryer, don't be afraid to get creative in the kitchen - try new spices, coat your food with tasty breading, and don't forget to flip! And when it comes time to clean up, just remember - a clean air fryer is a happy air fryer.

In the end, the air fryer is more than just a cooking appliance - it's a lifestyle. So embrace it, love it, and most importantly, cook with it. Who knows? You might just become the air fryer guru among your friends and family.

So go ahead and take the plunge - it's time to join the air fryer revolution. Your taste buds (and your waistline) will thank you!

# Chapter 1
## Breakfasts

# Chapter 1 Breakfasts

## Gluten-Free Granola Cereal

**Prep time: 7 minutes | Cook time: 30 minutes | Makes 820 ml**

| | |
|---|---|
| Oil, for spraying | 60 ml maple syrup or honey |
| 350 g gluten-free porridge oats | 1 tablespoon toasted sesame oil or vegetable oil |
| 120 g chopped walnuts | 1 teaspoon ground cinnamon |
| 120 g chopped almonds | ½ teaspoon salt |
| 120 g pumpkin seeds | 120 g dried cranberries |

1. Preheat the air fryer to 120°C. Line the air fryer basket with parchment and spray lightly with oil. (Do not skip the step of lining the basket; the parchment will keep the granola from falling through the holes.) 2. In a large bowl, mix together the oats, walnuts, almonds, pumpkin seeds, maple syrup, sesame oil, cinnamon, and salt. 3. Spread the mixture in an even layer in the prepared basket. 4. Cook for 30 minutes, stirring every 10 minutes. 5. Transfer the granola to a bowl, add the dried cranberries, and toss to combine. 6. Let cool to room temperature before storing in an airtight container.

## Peppered Maple Bacon Knots

**Prep time: 5 minutes | Cook time: 7 to 8 minutes | Serves 6**

| | |
|---|---|
| 450 g maple smoked/cured bacon rashers | 48 g soft brown sugar |
| 60 ml maple syrup | Coarsely cracked black peppercorns, to taste |

1. Preheat the air fryer to 200°C. 2. On a clean work surface, tie each bacon strip in a loose knot. 3. Stir together the maple syrup and soft brown sugar in a bowl. Generously brush this mixture over the bacon knots. 4. Working in batches, arrange the bacon knots in the air fryer basket. Sprinkle with the coarsely cracked black peppercorns. 5. Air fry for 5 minutes. Flip the bacon knots and continue cooking for 2 to 3 minutes more, or until the bacon is crisp. 6. Remove from the basket to a paper towel-lined plate. Repeat with the remaining bacon knots. 7. Let the bacon knots cool for a few minutes and serve warm.

## Chimichanga Breakfast Burrito

**Prep time: 10 minutes | Cook time: 10 minutes | Serves 2**

| | |
|---|---|
| 2 large (10- to 12-inch) wheat tortillas | 4 corn tortilla chips, crushed |
| 120 g canned refried beans (pinto or black work equally well) | 120 g grated chili cheese |
| | 12 pickled jalapeño slices |
| | 1 tablespoon vegetable oil |
| 4 large eggs, cooked scrambled | Guacamole, tomato salsa, and sour cream, for serving (optional) |

1. Place the tortillas on a work surface and divide the refried beans between them, spreading them in a rough rectangle in the center of the tortillas. Top the beans with the scrambled eggs, crushed chips, cheese, and jalapeños. Fold one side over the fillings, then fold in each short side and roll up the rest of the way like a burrito. 2. Brush the outside of the burritos with the oil, then transfer to the air fryer, seam-side down. Air fry at 180°C until the tortillas are browned and crisp and the filling is warm throughout, about 10 minutes. 3. Transfer the chimichangas to plates and serve warm with guacamole, tomato salsa, and sour cream, if you like.

## Southwestern Ham Egg Cups

**Prep time: 5 minutes | Cook time: 12 minutes | Serves 2**

| | |
|---|---|
| 4 (30 g) slices wafer-thin ham | pepper |
| 4 large eggs | 2 tablespoons diced brown onion |
| 2 tablespoons full-fat sour cream | 120 g grated medium Cheddar cheese |
| 60 g diced green pepper | |
| 2 tablespoons diced red | |

1. Place one slice of ham on the bottom of four baking cups. 2. In a large bowl, whisk eggs with sour cream. Stir in green pepper, red pepper, and onion. 3. Pour the egg mixture into ham-lined baking cups. Top with Cheddar. Place cups into the air fryer basket. 4. Adjust the temperature to 160°C and bake for 12 minutes or until the tops are browned. 5. Serve warm.

## Egg Tarts

**Prep time: 10 minutes | Cook time: 17 to 20 minutes | Makes 2 tarts**

| | |
|---|---|
| ⅓ sheet frozen puff pastry, thawed | 2 eggs |
| Cooking oil spray | ¼ teaspoon salt, divided |
| 120 g grated Cheddar cheese | 1 teaspoon minced fresh parsley (optional) |

1. Insert the crisper plate into the basket and the basket into the unit. Preheat the unit by selecting BAKE, setting the temperature to 200ºC, and setting the time to 3 minutes. Select START/STOP to begin. 2. Lay the puff pastry sheet on a piece of parchment paper and cut it in half. 3. Once the unit is preheated, spray the crisper plate with cooking oil. Transfer the 2 squares of pastry to the basket, keeping them on the parchment paper. 4. Select BAKE, set the temperature to 200ºC, and set the time to 20 minutes. Select START/STOP to begin. 5. After 10 minutes, use a metal spoon to press down the center of each pastry square to make a well. Divide the cheese equally between the baked pastries. Carefully crack an egg on top of the cheese, and sprinkle each with the salt. Resume cooking for 7 to 10 minutes. 6. When the cooking is complete, the eggs will be cooked through. Sprinkle each with parsley (if using) and serve.

## Honey-Apricot Granola with Greek Yoghurt

**Prep time: 10 minutes | Cook time: 30 minutes | Serves 6**

| | |
|---|---|
| 235 g porridge oats | 1 tablespoon rapeseed oil |
| 60 g dried apricots, diced | 1 teaspoon ground cinnamon |
| 60 g almond slivers | ¼ teaspoon ground nutmeg |
| 60 g walnuts, chopped | ¼ teaspoon salt |
| 60 g pumpkin seeds | 2 tablespoons sugar-free dark chocolate chips (optional) |
| 60 to 80 ml honey, plus more for drizzling | 700 ml fat-free natural yoghurt |

1. Preheat the air fryer to 130ºC. Line the air fryer basket with parchment paper. 2. In a large bowl, combine the oats, apricots, almonds, walnuts, pumpkin seeds, honey, rapeseed oil, cinnamon, nutmeg, and salt, mixing so that the honey, oil, and spices are well distributed. 3. Pour the mixture onto the parchment paper and spread it into an even layer. 4. Bake for 10 minutes, then shake or stir and spread back out into an even layer. Continue baking for 10 minutes more, then repeat the process of shaking or stirring the mixture. Bake for an additional 10 minutes before removing from the air fryer. 5. Allow the granola to cool completely before stirring in the chocolate chips (if using) and pouring into an airtight container for storage. 6. For each serving, top 120 ml Greek yoghurt with 80 ml granola and a drizzle of honey, if needed.

## Onion Omelette

**Prep time: 10 minutes | Cook time: 12 minutes | Serves 2**

| | |
|---|---|
| 3 eggs | 1 large onion, chopped |
| Salt and ground black pepper, to taste | 2 tablespoons grated Cheddar cheese |
| ½ teaspoons soy sauce | Cooking spray |

1. Preheat the air fryer to 180ºC. 2. In a bowl, whisk together the eggs, salt, pepper, and soy sauce. 3. Spritz a small pan with cooking spray. Spread the chopped onion across the bottom of the pan, then transfer the pan to the air fryer. 4. Bake in the preheated air fryer for 6 minutes or until the onion is translucent. 5. Add the egg mixture on top of the onions to coat well. Add the cheese on top, then continue baking for another 6 minutes. 6. Allow to cool before serving.

## Maple Granola

**Prep time: 5 minutes | Cook time: 40 minutes | Makes 475 ml**

| | |
|---|---|
| 235 g porridge oats | oil, such as refined coconut or sunflower |
| 3 tablespoons pure maple syrup | ¼ teaspoon sea salt |
| 1 tablespoon sugar | ¼ teaspoon ground cinnamon |
| 1 tablespoon neutral-flavoured | ¼ teaspoon vanilla extract |

1. Insert the crisper plate into the basket and the basket into the unit. Preheat the unit by selecting BAKE, setting the temperature to 120ºC, and setting the time to 3 minutes. Select START/STOP to begin. 2. In a medium bowl, stir together the oats, maple syrup, sugar, oil, salt, cinnamon, and vanilla until thoroughly combined. Transfer the granola to a 6-by-2-inch round baking pan. 3. Once the unit is preheated, place the pan into the basket. 4. Select BAKE, set the temperature to 120ºC and set the time to 40 minutes. Select START/STOP to begin. 5. After 10 minutes, stir the granola well. Resume cooking, stirring the granola every 10 minutes, for a total of 40 minutes, or until the granola is lightly browned and mostly dry. 6. When the cooking is complete, place the granola on a plate to cool. It will become crisp as it cools. Store the completely cooled granola in an airtight container in a cool, dry place for 1 to 2 weeks.

## Spinach and Mushroom Mini Quiche

**Prep time: 10 minutes | Cook time: 15 minutes | Serves 4**

| | |
|---|---|
| 1 teaspoon rapeseed oil, plus more for spraying | 4 eggs, beaten |
| 235 g roughly chopped mushrooms | 120 g grated Cheddar cheese |
| 235 g fresh baby spinach, grated | 120 g grated Cheddar cheese |
| | ¼ teaspoon salt |
| | ¼ teaspoon black pepper |

1. Spray 4 silicone baking cups with rapeseed oil and set aside. 2. In a medium sauté pan over medium heat, warm 1 teaspoon of rapeseed oil. Add the mushrooms and sauté until soft, 3 to 4 minutes. 3. Add the spinach and cook until wilted, 1 to 2 minutes. Set aside. 4. In a medium bowl, whisk together the eggs, Cheddar cheese, Cheddar cheese, salt, and pepper. 5. Gently fold the mushrooms and spinach into the egg mixture. 6. Pour ¼ of the mixture into each silicone baking cup. 7. Place the baking cups into the air fryer basket and air fry at 180ºC for 5 minutes. Stir the mixture in each ramekin slightly and air fry until the egg has set, an additional 3 to 5 minutes.

## Breakfast Cobbler

**Prep time: 20 minutes | Cook time: 30 minutes | Serves 4**

| | |
|---|---|
| Filling: | Biscuits: |
| 280 g sausage meat, crumbled | 3 large egg whites |
| 60 g minced onions | 90 g blanched almond flour |
| 2 cloves garlic, minced | 1 teaspoon baking powder |
| ½ teaspoon fine sea salt | ¼ teaspoon fine sea salt |
| ½ teaspoon ground black pepper | 2½ tablespoons very cold unsalted butter, cut into ¼-inch pieces |
| 1 (230 g) package soft cheese (or soft cheese style spread for dairy-free), softened | Fresh thyme leaves, for garnish |
| 180 g beef or chicken stock | |

1. Preheat the air fryer to 200ºC. 2. Place the sausage, onions, and garlic in a pie pan. Using your hands, break up the sausage into small pieces and spread it evenly throughout the pie pan. Season with the salt and pepper. Place the pan in the air fryer and bake for 5 minutes. 3. While the sausage cooks, place the soft cheese and stock in a food processor or blender and purée until smooth. 4. Remove the pork from the air fryer and use a fork or metal spatula to crumble it more. Pour the soft cheese mixture into the sausage and stir to combine. Set aside. 5. Make the biscuits: Place the egg whites in a medium-sized mixing bowl or the bowl of a stand mixer and whip with a hand mixer or stand mixer until stiff peaks form. 6. In a separate medium-sized bowl, whisk together the almond flour, baking powder, and salt, then cut in the butter. When you are done, the mixture should still have chunks of butter. Gently fold the flour mixture into the egg whites with a rubber spatula. 7. Use a large spoon or ice cream scoop to scoop the dough into 4 equal-sized biscuits, making sure the butter is evenly distributed. Place the biscuits on top of the sausage and cook in the air fryer for 5 minutes, then turn the heat down to 160ºC and bake for another 17 to 20 minutes, until the biscuits are golden brown. Serve garnished with fresh thyme leaves. 8. Store leftovers in an airtight container in the refrigerator for up to 3 days. Reheat in a preheated 180ºC air fryer for 5 minutes, or until warmed through.

## Super Easy Bacon Cups

**Prep time: 5 minutes | Cook time: 20 minutes | Serves 2**

| | |
|---|---|
| 3 slices bacon, cooked, sliced in half | 2 teaspoons grated Parmesan cheese |
| 2 slices ham | Salt and ground black pepper, to taste |
| 1 slice tomato | |
| 2 eggs | |

1. Preheat the air fryer to 190ºC. Line 2 greased muffin tins with 3 half-strips of bacon 2. Put one slice of ham and half slice of tomato in each muffin tin on top of the bacon 3. Crack one egg on top of the tomato in each muffin tin and sprinkle each with half a teaspoon of grated Parmesan cheese. Sprinkle with salt and ground black pepper, if desired. 4. Bake in the preheated air fryer for 20 minutes. Remove from the air fryer and let cool. 5. Serve warm.

## Tomato and Mozzarella Bruschetta

**Prep time: 5 minutes | Cook time: 4 minutes | Serves 1**

| | |
|---|---|
| 6 small loaf slices | 1 tablespoon fresh basil, chopped |
| 120 g tomatoes, finely chopped | 1 tablespoon rapeseed oil |
| 85 g Cheddar cheese, grated | |

1. Preheat the air fryer to 180ºC. 2. Put the loaf slices inside the air fryer and air fry for about 3 minutes. 3. Add the tomato, Mozzarella, basil, and rapeseed oil on top. 4. Air fry for an additional minute before serving.

## Quick and Easy Blueberry Muffins

**Prep time: 10 minutes | Cook time: 12 minutes | Makes 8 muffins**

| | |
|---|---|
| 160 g flour | 1 egg |
| 96 g sugar | 120 ml milk |
| 2 teaspoons baking powder | 160 g blueberries, fresh or frozen and thawed |
| ¼ teaspoon salt | |
| 80 ml rapeseed oil | |

1. Preheat the air fryer to 170ºC. 2. In a medium bowl, stir together flour, sugar, baking powder, and salt. 3. In a separate bowl, combine oil, egg, and milk and mix well. 4. Add egg mixture to dry ingredients and stir just until moistened. 5. Gently stir in the blueberries. 6. Spoon batter evenly into parchment paper-lined muffin cups. 7. Put 4 muffin cups in air fryer basket and bake for 12 minutes or until tops spring back when touched lightly. 8. Repeat previous step to bake remaining muffins. 9. Serve immediately.

## Egg White Cups

**Prep time: 10 minutes | Cook time: 15 minutes | Serves 4**

| | |
|---|---|
| 475 ml 100% liquid egg whites | ¼ teaspoon onion granules |
| 3 tablespoons salted butter, melted | ½ medium plum tomato, cored and diced |
| ¼ teaspoon salt | 120 g chopped fresh spinach leaves |

1. In a large bowl, whisk egg whites with butter, salt, and onion granules. Stir in tomato and spinach, then pour evenly into four ramekins greased with cooking spray. 2. Place ramekins into air fryer basket. Adjust the temperature to 150ºC and bake for 15 minutes. Eggs will be fully cooked and firm in the center when done. Serve warm.

## Canadian Bacon Muffin Sandwiches

**Prep time: 5 minutes | Cook time: 8 minutes | Serves 4**

| | |
|---|---|
| 4 muffins, split | 4 slices cheese |
| 8 slices back bacon | Cooking spray |

1. Preheat the air fryer to 190ºC. 2. Make the sandwiches: Top each of 4 muffin halves with 2 slices of bacon, 1 slice of cheese, and finish with the remaining muffin half. 3. Put the sandwiches in the air fryer basket and spritz the tops with cooking spray. 4. Bake for 4 minutes. Flip the sandwiches and bake for another 4 minutes. 5. Divide the sandwiches among four plates and serve warm.

## Egg in a Hole

**Prep time: 5 minutes | Cook time: 5 minutes | Serves 1**

| | |
|---|---|
| 1 slice bread | 1 tablespoon grated Cheddar cheese |
| 1 teaspoon butter, softened | 2 teaspoons diced gammon |
| 1 egg | |
| Salt and pepper, to taste | |

1. Preheat the air fryer to 170ºC. Place a baking dish in the air fryer basket. 2. On a flat work surface, cut a hole in the center of the bread slice with a 2½-inch-diameter biscuit cutter. 3. Spread the butter evenly on each side of the bread slice and transfer to the baking dish. 4. Crack the egg into the hole and season as desired with salt and pepper. Scatter the grated cheese and diced gammon on top. 5. Bake in the preheated air fryer for 5 minutes until the bread is lightly browned and the egg is cooked to your preference. 6. Remove from the basket and serve hot.

## Butternut Squash and Ricotta Frittata

**Prep time: 10 minutes | Cook time: 33 minutes | Serves 2 to 3**

| | |
|---|---|
| 235 ml cubed (½-inch) butternut squash (160 g) | 4 fresh sage leaves, thinly sliced |
| 2 tablespoons rapeseed oil | 6 large eggs, lightly beaten |
| Coarse or flaky salt and freshly ground black pepper, to taste | 120 g ricotta cheese |
| | Cayenne pepper |

1. In a bowl, toss the squash with the rapeseed oil and season with salt and black pepper until evenly coated. Sprinkle the sage on the bottom of a cake pan and place the squash on top. Place the pan in the air fryer and bake at 200ºC for 10 minutes. Stir to incorporate the sage, then cook until the squash is tender and lightly caramelized at the edges, about 3 minutes more. 2. Pour the eggs over the squash, dollop the ricotta all over, and sprinkle with cayenne. Bake at 150ºC until the eggs are set and the frittata is golden brown on top, about 20 minutes. Remove the pan from the air fryer and cut the frittata into wedges to serve.

## Spinach and Swiss Frittata with Mushrooms

**Prep time: 10 minutes | Cook time: 20 minutes | Serves 4**

| rapeseed oil cooking spray | 110 g baby mushrooms, sliced |
| 8 large eggs | 1 shallot, diced |
| ½ teaspoon salt | 120 g grated Swiss cheese, divided |
| ½ teaspoon black pepper | Hot sauce, for serving (optional) |
| 1 garlic clove, minced | |
| 475 g fresh baby spinach | |

1. Preheat the air fryer to 180ºC. Lightly coat the inside of a 6-inch round cake pan with rapeseed oil cooking spray. 2. In a large bowl, beat the eggs, salt, pepper, and garlic for 1 to 2 minutes, or until well combined. 3. Fold in the spinach, mushrooms, shallot, and 60 ml the Swiss cheese. 4. Pour the egg mixture into the prepared cake pan, and sprinkle the remaining 60 ml Swiss over the top. 5. Place into the air fryer and bake for 18 to 20 minutes, or until the eggs are set in the center. 6. Remove from the air fryer and allow to cool for 5 minutes. Drizzle with hot sauce (if using) before serving.

## Berry Muffins

**Prep time: 15 minutes | Cook time: 12 to 17 minutes | Makes 8 muffins**

| 160 g plus 1 tablespoon plain flour, divided | 2 teaspoons baking powder |
| 48 g granulated sugar | 2 eggs |
| 2 tablespoons light soft brown sugar | 160 ml whole milk |
| | 80 ml neutral oil |
| | 235 g mixed fresh berries |

1. In a medium bowl, stir together 315 g of flour, the granulated sugar, soft brown sugar, and baking powder until mixed well. 2. In a small bowl, whisk the eggs, milk, and oil until combined. Stir the egg mixture into the dry ingredients just until combined. 3. In another small bowl, toss the mixed berries with the remaining 1 tablespoon of flour until coated. Gently stir the berries into the batter. 4. Double up 16 foil muffin cups to make 8 cups. 5. Insert the crisper plate into the basket and the basket into the unit. Preheat the unit by selecting BAKE, setting the temperature to 160ºC, and setting the time to 3 minutes. Select START/STOP to begin. 6. Once the unit is preheated, place 1 L into the basket and fill each three-quarters full with the batter. 7. Select BAKE, set the temperature to 160ºC, and set the time for 17 minutes. Select START/STOP to begin. 8. After about 12 minutes, check the muffins. If they spring back when lightly touched with your finger, they are done. If not, resume cooking. 9. When the cooking is done, transfer the muffins to a wire rack to cool. 10. Repeat steps 6, 7, and 8 with the remaining muffin cups and batter. 11. Let the muffins cool for 10 minutes before serving.

## French Toast Sticks

**Prep time: 10 minutes | Cook time: 9 minutes | Serves 4**

| Oil, for spraying | 1 teaspoon ground cinnamon |
| 6 large eggs | 8 slices bread, cut into thirds |
| 315 ml milk | Syrup of choice, for serving |
| 2 teaspoons vanilla extract | |

1. Preheat the air fryer to 190ºC. Line the air fryer basket with parchment and spray lightly with oil. 2. In a shallow bowl, whisk the eggs, milk, vanilla, and cinnamon. 3. Dunk one piece of bread in the egg mixture, making sure to coat both sides. Work quickly so the bread doesn't get soggy. Immediately transfer the bread to the prepared basket. 4. Repeat with the remaining bread, making sure the pieces don't touch each other. You may need to work in batches, depending on the size of your air fryer. 5. Air fry for 5 minutes, flip, and cook for another 3 to 4 minutes, until browned and crispy. 6. Serve immediately with your favourite syrup.

## Homemade Toaster Pastries

**Prep time: 10 minutes | Cook time: 11 minutes | Makes 6 pastries**

| Oil, for spraying | 340 g icing sugar |
| 1 (425 g) package ready-to-roll pie crust | 3 tablespoons milk |
| 6 tablespoons jam or preserves of choice | 1 to 2 tablespoons sprinkles of choice |

1. Preheat the air fryer to 180ºC. Line the air fryer basket with parchment and lightly spray with oil. 2. Cut the pie crust into 12 rectangles, about 3 by 4 inches each. You will need to reroll the dough scraps to get 12 rectangles. 3. Spread 1 tablespoon of jam in the centre of 6 rectangles, leaving ¼ inch around the edges. 4. Pour some water into a small bowl. Use your finger to moisten the edge of each rectangle. 5. Top each rectangle with another and use your fingers to press around the edges. Using the prongs of a fork, seal the edges of the dough and poke a few holes in the top of each one. Place the pastries in the prepared basket. 6. Air fry for 11 minutes. Let cool completely. 7. In a medium bowl, whisk together the icing sugar and milk. Spread the icing over the tops of the pastries and add sprinkles. Serve immediately.

## Simple Scotch Eggs

**Prep time: 5 minutes | Cook time: 25 minutes | Serves 4**

4 large hard boiled eggs
1 (340 g) package pork sausage meat
8 slices streaky bacon
4 wooden cocktail sticks, soaked in water for at least 30 minutes

1. Slice the sausage meat into four parts and place each part into a large circle. 2. Put an egg into each circle and wrap it in the sausage. Put in the refrigerator for 1 hour. 3. Preheat the air fryer to 230°C. 4. Make a cross with two pieces of streaky bacon. Put a wrapped egg in the center, fold the bacon over top of the egg, and secure with a toothpick. 5. Air fry in the preheated air fryer for 25 minutes. 6. Serve immediately.

## Breakfast Sammies

**Prep time: 15 minutes | Cook time: 20 minutes | Serves 5**

Biscuits:
6 large egg whites
240 g blanched almond flour, plus more if needed
1½ teaspoons baking powder
½ teaspoon fine sea salt
60 g (½ stick) very cold unsalted butter (or lard for dairy-free), cut into ¼-inch pieces
Eggs:
5 large eggs
½ teaspoon fine sea salt
¼ teaspoon ground black pepper
5 (30 g) slices Cheddar cheese (omit for dairy-free)
10 thin slices ham

1. Spray the air fryer basket with avocado oil. Preheat the air fryer to 180°C. Grease two pie pans or two baking pans that will fit inside your air fryer. 2. Make the biscuits: In a medium-sized bowl, whip the egg whites with a hand mixer until very stiff. Set aside. 3. In a separate medium-sized bowl, stir together the almond flour, baking powder, and salt until well combined. Cut in the butter. Gently fold the flour mixture into the egg whites with a rubber spatula. If the dough is too wet to form into mounds, add a few tablespoons of almond flour until the dough holds together well. 4. Using a large spoon, divide the dough into 5 equal portions and drop them about 1 inch apart on one of the greased pie pans. (If you're using a smaller air fryer, work in batches if necessary.) Place the pan in the air fryer and bake for 11 to 14 minutes, until the biscuits are golden brown. Remove from the air fryer and set aside to cool. 5. Make the eggs: Set the air fryer to 190°C. Crack the eggs into the remaining greased pie pan and sprinkle with the salt and pepper. Place the eggs in the air fryer to bake for 5 minutes, or until they are cooked to your liking. 6. Open the air fryer and top each egg yolk with a slice of cheese (if using). Bake for another minute, or until the cheese is melted. 7. Once the biscuits are cool, slice them in half lengthwise. Place 1 cooked egg topped with cheese and 2 slices of ham in each biscuit. 8. Store leftover biscuits, eggs, and ham in separate airtight containers in the fridge for up to 3 days. Reheat the biscuits and eggs on a baking sheet in a preheated 180°C air fryer for 5 minutes, or until warmed through.

## Spinach Omelet

**Prep time: 5 minutes | Cook time: 12 minutes | Serves 2**

4 large eggs
350 g chopped fresh spinach leaves
2 tablespoons peeled and chopped brown onion
2 tablespoons salted butter, melted
120 g grated mild Cheddar cheese
¼ teaspoon salt

1. In an ungreased round nonstick baking dish, whisk eggs. Stir in spinach, onion, butter, Cheddar, and salt. 2. Place dish into air fryer basket. Adjust the temperature to 160°C and bake for 12 minutes. Omelet will be done when browned on the top and firm in the middle. 3. Slice in half and serve warm on two medium plates.

## BLT Breakfast Wrap

**Prep time: 5 minutes | Cook time: 10 minutes | Serves 4**

230 g reduced-salt bacon
8 tablespoons mayonnaise
8 large romaine lettuce leaves
4 vine tomatoes, sliced
Salt and freshly ground black pepper, to taste

1. Arrange the bacon in a single layer in the air fryer basket. (It's OK if the bacon sits a bit on the sides.) Set the air fryer to 180°C and air fry for 10 minutes. Check for crispiness and air fry for 2 to 3 minutes longer if needed. Cook in batches, if necessary, and drain the grease in between batches. 2. Spread 1 tablespoon of mayonnaise on each of the lettuce leaves and top with the tomatoes and cooked bacon. Season to taste with salt and freshly ground black pepper. Roll the lettuce leaves as you would a burrito, securing with a toothpick if desired.

# Chapter 2
## Family Favorites

# Chapter 2 Family Favorites

## Scallops with Green Vegetables

**Prep time: 15 minutes | Cook time: 8 to 11 minutes | Serves 4**

| | |
|---|---|
| 235 g green beans | ½ teaspoon dried basil |
| 235 g garden peas | ½ teaspoon dried oregano |
| 235 g frozen chopped broccoli | 340 g sea scallops |
| 2 teaspoons olive oil | |

1. In a large bowl, toss the green beans, peas, and broccoli with the olive oil. 2. Place in the air fryer basket. 3. Air fry at 200°C for 4 to 6 minutes, or until the vegetables are crisp-tender. 4. Remove the vegetables from the air fryer basket and sprinkle with the herbs. Set aside. 5. In the air fryer basket, put the scallops and air fry for 4 to 5 minutes, or until the scallops are firm and reach an internal temperature of just 64°C on a meat thermometer. 6. Toss scallops with the vegetables and serve immediately.

## Puffed Egg Tarts

**Prep time: 10 minutes | Cook time: 42 minutes | Makes 4 tarts**

| | |
|---|---|
| Oil, for spraying | 4 large eggs |
| Plain flour, for dusting | 2 teaspoons chopped fresh parsley |
| 1 (340 g) sheet frozen puff pastry, thawed | Salt and ground black pepper, to taste |
| 180 g shredded Cheddar cheese, divided | |

1. Preheat the air fryer to 200°C. 2. Line the air fryer basket with parchment and spray lightly with oil. Lightly dust your work surface with flour. 3. Unfold the puff pastry and cut it into 4 equal squares. 4. Place 2 squares in the prepared basket. Cook for 10 minutes. 5. Remove the basket. Press the centre of each tart shell with a spoon to make an indentation. 6. Sprinkle 3 tablespoons of cheese into each indentation and crack 1 egg into the centre of each tart shell. 7. Cook for another 7 to 11 minutes, or until the eggs are cooked to your desired doneness. 8. Repeat with the remaining puff pastry squares, cheese, and eggs. 9. Sprinkle evenly with the parsley, and season with salt and black pepper. 10. Serve immediately.

## Cajun Shrimp

**Prep time: 15 minutes | Cook time: 9 minutes | Serves 4**

| | |
|---|---|
| Oil, for spraying | ½ medium yellow squash or butternut squash, cut into ¼-inch-thick slices |
| 450 g king prawns, peeled and deveined | |
| 1 tablespoon Cajun seasoning | 1 green pepper, seeded and cut into 1-inch pieces |
| 170 g Polish sausage, cut into thick slices | 2 tablespoons olive oil |
| ½ medium courgette, cut into ¼-inch-thick slices | ½ teaspoon salt |

1. Preheat the air fryer to 200°C. 2. Line the air fryer basket with parchment and spray lightly with oil. In a large bowl, toss together the shrimp and Cajun seasoning. 3. Add the kielbasa, courgette, squash, pepper, olive oil, and salt and mix well. 4. Transfer the mixture to the prepared basket, taking care not to overcrowd. 5. You may need to work in batches, depending on the size of your air fryer. 6. Cook for 9 minutes, shaking and stirring every 3 minutes. 7. Serve immediately.

## Steak and Vegetable Kebabs

**Prep time: 15 minutes | Cook time: 5 to 7 minutes | Serves 4**

| | |
|---|---|
| 2 tablespoons balsamic vinegar | 340 g silverside, cut into 1-inch pieces |
| 2 teaspoons olive oil | 1 red pepper, sliced |
| ½ teaspoon dried marjoram | 16 button mushrooms |
| ⅛ teaspoon ground black pepper | 235 g cherry tomatoes |

1. In a medium bowl, stir together the balsamic vinegar, olive oil, marjoram, and black pepper. 2. Add the steak and stir to coat. Let stand for 10 minutes at room temperature. 3. Alternating items, thread the beef, red pepper, mushrooms, and tomatoes onto 8 bamboo or metal skewers that fit in the air fryer. 4. Air fry at 200°C for 5 to 7 minutes, or until the beef is browned and reaches at least 64°C on a meat thermometer. 5. Serve immediately.

## Pork Burgers with Red Cabbage Salad

**Prep time: 20 minutes | Cook time: 7 to 9 minutes | Serves 4**

| | |
|---|---|
| 120 ml Greek yoghurt | pork |
| 2 tablespoons low-salt mustard, divided | ½ teaspoon paprika |
| 1 tablespoon lemon juice | 235 g mixed salad leaves |
| 60 g sliced red cabbage | 2 small tomatoes, sliced |
| 60 g grated carrots | 8 small low-salt wholemeal sandwich buns, cut in half |
| 450 g lean finely chopped | |

1. In a small bowl, combine the yoghurt, 1 tablespoon mustard, lemon juice, cabbage, and carrots; mix and refrigerate. 2.In a medium bowl, combine the pork, remaining 1 tablespoon mustard, and paprika. Form into 8 small patties. Put the sliders into the air fryer basket. 3.Air fry at 200ºC for 7 to 9 minutes, or until the sliders register 74ºC as tested with a meat thermometer. 4.Assemble the burgers by placing some of the lettuce greens on a bun bottom. 5.Top with a tomato slice, the burgers, and the cabbage mixture. 6.Add the bun top and serve immediately.

## Pecan Rolls

**Prep time: 20 minutes | Cook time: 20 to 24 minutes | Makes 12 rolls**

| | |
|---|---|
| 220 g plain flour, plus more for dusting | 180 ml milk, whole or semi-skimmed |
| 2 tablespoons caster sugar, plus 60 ml, divided | 40 g packed light muscovado sugar |
| 1 teaspoon salt | 120g chopped pecans, toasted |
| 3 tablespoons butter, at room temperature | 1 to 2 tablespoons oil |
| | 35g icing sugar (optional) |

1. In a large bowl, whisk the flour, 2 tablespoons caster sugar, and salt until blended. 2.Stir in the butter and milk briefly until a sticky dough form. In a small bowl, stir together the brown sugar and remaining 60 g caster sugar. 3.Place a piece of parchment paper on a work surface and dust it with flour. Roll the dough on the prepared surface to ¼ inch thickness. 4.Spread the sugar mixture over the dough. Sprinkle the pecans on top. Roll up the dough jelly roll-style, pinching the ends to seal. 5.Cut the dough into 12 rolls. Preheat the air fryer to 160ºC. 6.Line the air fryer basket with parchment paper and spritz the parchment with oil. Place 6 rolls on the prepared parchment. Bake for 5 minutes. 7.Flip the rolls and bake for 5 to 7 minutes more until lightly browned. Repeat with the remaining rolls. 8.Sprinkle with icing sugar (if using).

## Fried Green Tomatoes

**Prep time: 15 minutes | Cook time: 6 to 8 minutes | Serves 4**

| | |
|---|---|
| 4 medium green tomatoes | 120 g Japanese breadcrumbs |
| 50 g plain flour | 2 teaspoons olive oil |
| 2 egg whites | 1 teaspoon paprika |
| 60 ml almond milk | 1 clove garlic, minced |
| 235 g ground almonds | |

1. Rinse the tomatoes and pat dry. 2.Cut the tomatoes into ½-inch slices, discarding the thinner ends. Put the flour on a plate. 3.In a shallow bowl, beat the egg whites with the almond milk until frothy. 4.And on another plate, combine the almonds, breadcrumbs, olive oil, paprika, and garlic and mix well. 5.Dip the tomato slices into the flour, then into the egg white mixture, then into the almond mixture to coat. 6.Place four of the coated tomato slices in the air fryer basket. 7.Air fry at 200ºC for 6 to 8 minutes or until the tomato coating is crisp and golden brown. 8.Repeat with remaining tomato slices and serve immediately.

## Churro Bites

**Prep time: 5 minutes | Cook time: 6 minutes | Makes 36 bites**

| | |
|---|---|
| Oil, for spraying | 1 tablespoon ground cinnamon |
| 1 (500 g) package frozen puffed pastry, thawed | 90 g icing sugar |
| 180 g caster sugar | 1 tablespoon milk |

1. Preheat the air fryer to 200ºC. 2.Line the air fryer basket with parchment and spray lightly with oil. 3.Unfold the puff pastry onto a clean work surface. Using a sharp knife, cut the dough into 36 bite-size pieces. 4.Place the dough pieces in one layer in the prepared basket, taking care not to let the pieces touch or overlap. 5.Cook for 3 minutes, flip, and cook for another 3 minutes, or until puffed and golden. In a small bowl, mix together the caster sugar and cinnamon. 6.In another small bowl, whisk together the icing sugar and milk. 7.Dredge the bites in the cinnamon-sugar mixture until evenly coated. 8.Serve with the icing on the side for dipping.

# Mixed Berry Crumble

**Prep time: 10 minutes | Cook time: 11 to 16 minutes | Serves 4**

- 120 g chopped fresh strawberries
- 120 g fresh blueberries
- 80 g frozen raspberries
- 1 tablespoon freshly squeezed lemon juice
- 1 tablespoon honey
- 80 g wholemeal plain flour
- 3 tablespoons light muscovado sugar
- 2 tablespoons unsalted butter, melted

1. In a baking pan, combine the strawberries, blueberries, and raspberries. 2. Drizzle with the lemon juice and honey. 3. In a small bowl, mix the pastry flour and brown sugar. 4. Stir in the butter and mix until crumbly. 5. Sprinkle this mixture over the fruit. 6. Bake at 190°C for 11 to 16 minutes, or until the fruit is tender and bubbly and the topping is golden brown. 7. Serve warm.

# Meringue Cookies

**Prep time: 15 minutes | Cook time: 1 hour 30 minutes | Makes 20 cookies**

- Oil, for spraying
- 4 large egg whites
- 185 g sugar
- Pinch cream of tartar

1. Preheat the air fryer to 60°C. 2. Line the air fryer basket with parchment and spray lightly with oil. 3. In a small heatproof bowl, whisk together the egg whites and sugar. 4. Fill a small saucepan halfway with water, place it over medium heat, and bring to a light simmer. 5. Place the bowl with the egg whites on the saucepan, making sure the bottom of the bowl does not touch the water. 6. Whisk the mixture until the sugar is dissolved. Transfer the mixture to a large bowl and add the cream of tartar. 7. Using an electric mixer, beat the mixture on high until it is glossy and stiff peaks form. 8. Transfer the mixture to a piping bag or a zip-top plastic bag with a corner cut off. Pipe rounds into the prepared basket. 9. You may need to work in batches, depending on the size of your air fryer. Cook for 1 hour 30 minutes. 10. Turn off the air fryer and let the meringues cool completely inside. 11. The residual heat will continue to dry them out.

# Chapter 3
# Fast and Easy Everyday Favourites

# Chapter 3 Fast and Easy Everyday Favourites

## Crunchy Fried Okra

**Prep time: 5 minutes | Cook time: 8 to 10 minutes | Serves 4**

| | |
|---|---|
| 120 g self-raising yellow cornmeal (alternatively add 1 tablespoon baking powder to cornmeal) | 1 teaspoon salt |
| | ½ teaspoon freshly ground black pepper |
| 1 teaspoon Italian-style seasoning | 2 large eggs, beaten |
| | 475 g okra slices |
| 1 teaspoon paprika | Cooking spray |

1. Preheat the air fryer to 200ºC. 2.Line the air fryer basket with parchment paper. In a shallow bowl, whisk the cornmeal, Italian-style seasoning, paprika, salt, and pepper until blended. 3.Place the beaten eggs in a second shallow bowl. Add the okra to the beaten egg and stir to coat. 4.Add the egg and okra mixture to the cornmeal mixture and stir until coated. 5.Place the okra on the parchment and spritz it with oil. 6.Air fry for 4 minutes. Shake the basket, spritz the okra with oil, and air fry for 4 to 6 minutes more until lightly browned and crispy. 7.Serve immediately.

## Air Fried Butternut Squash with Chopped Hazelnuts

**Prep time: 10 minutes | Cook time: 20 minutes | Makes 700 ml**

| | |
|---|---|
| 2 tablespoons whole hazelnuts | ¼ teaspoon freshly ground black pepper |
| 700 g butternut squash, peeled, deseeded, and cubed | 2 teaspoons olive oil |
| ¼ teaspoon rock salt | Cooking spray |

1. Preheat the air fryer to 150ºC. 2.Spritz the air fryer basket with cooking spray. 3.Arrange the hazelnuts in the preheated air fryer. Air fry for 3 minutes or until soft. 4.Chopped the hazelnuts roughly and transfer to a small bowl. Set aside. 5.Set the air fryer temperature to 180ºC. 6.Spritz with cooking spray. Put the butternut squash in a large bowl, then sprinkle with salt and pepper and drizzle with olive oil. 7.Toss to coat well. Transfer the squash in the air fryer. Air fry for 20 minutes or until the squash is soft. 8.Shake the basket halfway through the frying time. 9.When the frying is complete, transfer the squash onto a plate and sprinkle with chopped hazelnuts before serving.

## Cheesy Chilli Toast

**Prep time: 5 minutes | Cook time: 5 minutes | Serves 1**

| | |
|---|---|
| 2 tablespoons grated Parmesan cheese | room temperature |
| | 10 to 15 thin slices serrano chilli or jalapeño |
| 2 tablespoons grated Mozzarella cheese | 2 slices sourdough bread |
| 2 teaspoons salted butter, at | ½ teaspoon black pepper |

1. Preheat the air fryer to 160ºC. 2.In a small bowl, stir together the Parmesan, Mozzarella, butter, and chillies. 3.Spread half the mixture onto one side of each slice of bread. 4.Sprinkle with the pepper. 5.Place the slices, cheese-side up, in the air fryer basket. 6.Bake for 5 minutes, or until the cheese has melted and started to brown slightly. 7.Serve immediately.

## Air Fried Shishito Peppers

**Prep time: 5 minutes | Cook time: 5 minutes | Serves 4**

| | |
|---|---|
| 230 g shishito or Padron peppers (about 24) | Coarse sea salt, to taste |
| | Lemon wedges, for serving |
| 1 tablespoon olive oil | Cooking spray |

1. Preheat the air fryer to 200ºC. 2.Spritz the air fryer basket with cooking spray. 3.Toss the peppers with olive oil in a large bowl to coat well. Arrange the peppers in the preheated air fryer. 4.Air fryer for 5 minutes or until blistered and lightly charred. Shake the basket and sprinkle the peppers with salt halfway through the cooking time. 5.Transfer the peppers onto a plate and squeeze the lemon wedges on top before serving.

## Corn Fritters

**Prep time: 15 minutes | Cook time: 8 minutes | Serves 6**

- 120 g self-raising flour
- 1 tablespoon sugar
- 1 teaspoon salt
- 1 large egg, lightly beaten
- 60 g buttermilk
- 180 g corn kernels
- 60 g minced onion
- Cooking spray

1. Preheat the air fryer to 180ºC. 2.Line the air fryer basket with parchment paper. In a medium bowl, whisk the flour, sugar, and salt until blended. Stir in the egg and buttermilk. 3.Add the corn and minced onion. 4.Mix well. Shape the corn fritter batter into 12 balls. 5.Place the fritters on the parchment and spritz with oil. Bake for 4 minutes. 6.Flip the fritters, spritz them with oil, and bake for 4 minutes more until firm and lightly browned. 7.Serve immediately.

## Air Fried Broccoli

**Prep time: 5 minutes | Cook time: 6 minutes | Serves 1**

- 4 egg yolks
- 60 g melted butter
- 240 g coconut flour
- Salt and pepper, to taste
- 475 g broccoli florets

1. Preheat the air fryer to 200ºC. In a bowl, whisk the egg yolks and melted butter together. 2.Throw in the coconut flour, salt and pepper, then stir again to combine well. 3.Dip each broccoli floret into the mixture and place in the air fryer basket. 4.Air fry for 6 minutes in batches if necessary. Take care when removing them from the air fryer and serve immediately.

## Buttery Sweet Potatoes

**Prep time: 5 minutes | Cook time: 10 minutes | Serves 4**

- 2 tablespoons melted butter
- 1 tablespoon light brown sugar
- 2 sweet potatoes, peeled and cut into ½-inch cubes
- Cooking spray

1. Preheat the air fryer to 200ºC. 2.Line the air fryer basket with parchment paper. In a medium bowl, stir together the melted butter and brown sugar until blended. 3.Toss the sweet potatoes in the butter mixture until coated. Place the sweet potatoes on the parchment and spritz with oil. 4.Air fry for 5 minutes. Shake the basket, spritz the sweet potatoes with oil, and air fry for 5 minutes more until they're soft enough to cut with a fork. 5.Serve immediately.

## Air Fried Tortilla Chips

**Prep time: 5 minutes | Cook time: 10 minutes | Serves 4**

- 4 six-inch corn tortillas, cut in half and slice into thirds
- 1 tablespoon rapeseed oil
- ¼ teaspoon rock salt
- Cooking spray

1. Preheat the air fryer to 180ºC. 2.Spritz the air fryer basket with cooking spray. 3.On a clean work surface, brush the tortilla chips with rapeseed oil, then transfer the chips in the preheated air fryer. 4.Air fry for 10 minutes or until crunchy and lightly browned. 5.Shake the basket and sprinkle with salt halfway through the cooking time. 6.Transfer the chips onto a plate lined with paper towels. 7.Serve immediately.

## Simple and Easy Croutons

**Prep time: 5 minutes | Cook time: 8 minutes | Serves 4**

- 2 sliced bread
- 1 tablespoon olive oil
- Hot soup, for serving

1. Preheat the air fryer to 200ºC. 2.Cut the slices of bread into medium-size chunks. 3.Brush the air fryer basket with the oil. 4.Place the chunks inside and air fry for at least 8 minutes. 5.Serve with hot soup.

## Spinach and Carrot Balls

**Prep time: 10 minutes | Cook time: 10 minutes | Serves 4**

- 2 slices toasted bread
- 1 carrot, peeled and grated
- 1 package fresh spinach, blanched and chopped
- ½ onion, chopped
- 1 egg, beaten
- ½ teaspoon garlic powder
- 1 teaspoon minced garlic
- 1 teaspoon salt
- ½ teaspoon black pepper
- 1 tablespoon Engevita yeast flakes
- 1 tablespoon flour

1. Preheat the air fryer to 200ºC. 2.In a food processor, pulse the toasted bread to form breadcrumbs. 3.Transfer into a shallow dish or bowl. In a bowl, mix together all the other ingredients. 4.Use your hands to shape the mixture into small-sized balls. 5.Roll the balls in the breadcrumbs, ensuring to cover them well. 6.Put in the air fryer basket and air fry for 10 minutes. 7.Serve immediately.

# Peppery Brown Rice Fritters

**Prep time: 10 minutes | Cook time: 8 to 10 minutes | Serves 4**

- 1 (284 g) bag frozen cooked brown rice, thawed
- 1 egg
- 3 tablespoons brown rice flour
- 80 g finely grated carrots
- 80 g minced red pepper
- 2 tablespoons minced fresh basil
- 3 tablespoons grated Parmesan cheese
- 2 teaspoons olive oil

1. Preheat the air fryer to 190°C. 2.In a small bowl, combine the thawed rice, egg, and flour and mix to blend. 3.Stir in the carrots, pepper, basil, and Parmesan cheese. 4.Form the mixture into 8 fritters and drizzle with the olive oil. 5.Put the fritters carefully into the air fryer basket. 6.Air fry for 8 to 10 minutes, or until the fritters are golden brown and cooked through. 7.Serve immediately.

# Herb-Roasted Veggies

**Prep time: 10 minutes | Cook time: 14 to 18 minutes | Serves 4**

- 1 red pepper, sliced
- 1 (230 g) package sliced mushrooms
- 235 g green beans, cut into 2-inch pieces
- 80 g diced red onion
- 3 garlic cloves, sliced
- 1 teaspoon olive oil
- ½ teaspoon dried basil
- ½ teaspoon dried tarragon

1. Preheat the air fryer to 180°C. 2.In a medium bowl, mix the red pepper, mushrooms, green beans, red onion, and garlic. 3.Drizzle with the olive oil. Toss to coat. 4.Add the herbs and toss again. Place the vegetables in the air fryer basket. 5.Roast for 14 to 18 minutes, or until tender. 6.Serve immediately.

# Chapter 4

# Poultry

# Chapter 4 Poultry

## Chicken Schnitzel Dogs

**Prep time: 15 minutes | Cook time: 8 to 10 minutes | Serves 4**

| | |
|---|---|
| 30 g flour | thin |
| ½ teaspoon salt | Oil for misting or cooking spray |
| 1 teaspoon marjoram | 4 whole-grain hotdog buns |
| 1 teaspoon dried parsley flakes | 4 slices Gouda cheese |
| ½ teaspoon thyme | 1 small Granny Smith apple, thinly sliced |
| 1 egg | 45 g shredded Swiss Chard cabbage |
| 1 teaspoon lemon juice | Coleslaw dressing |
| 1 teaspoon water | |
| 60 g bread crumbs | |
| 4 chicken tenders, pounded | |

1. In a shallow dish, mix together the flour, salt, marjoram, parsley, and thyme. 2. In another shallow dish, beat together egg, lemon juice, and water. 3. Place bread crumbs in a third shallow dish. 4. Cut each of the flattened chicken tenders in half lengthwise. 5. Dip flattened chicken strips in flour mixture, then egg wash. Let excess egg drip off and roll in bread crumbs. Spray both sides with oil or cooking spray. 6. Air fry at 200°C for 5 minutes. Spray with oil, turn over, and spray other side. 7. Cook for 3 to 5 minutes more, until well done and crispy brown. 8. To serve, place 2 schnitzel strips on bottom of each hotdog bun. Top with cheese, sliced apple, and cabbage. Drizzle with coleslaw dressing and top with other half of bun.

## Easy Turkey Tenderloin

**Prep time: 20 minutes | Cook time: 30 minutes | Serves 4**

| | |
|---|---|
| Olive oil | ½ teaspoon freshly ground black pepper |
| ½ teaspoon paprika | Pinch cayenne pepper |
| ½ teaspoon garlic powder | 680 g turkey breast tenderloin |
| ½ teaspoon salt | |

1. Spray the air fryer basket lightly with olive oil. 2. In a small bowl, combine the paprika, garlic powder, salt, black pepper, and cayenne pepper. Rub the mixture all over the turkey. 3. Place the turkey in the air fryer basket and lightly spray with olive oil. 4. Air fry at 190°C for 15 minutes. Flip the turkey over and lightly spray with olive oil. Air fry until the internal temperature reaches at least 80°C for an additional 10 to 15 minutes. 5. Let the turkey rest for 10 minutes before slicing and serving.

## Chicken Chimichangas

**Prep time: 20 minutes | Cook time: 8 to 10 minutes | Serves 4**

| | |
|---|---|
| 280 g cooked chicken, shredded | Oil for misting or cooking spray |
| 2 tablespoons chopped green chilies | Chimichanga Sauce: |
| ½ teaspoon oregano | 2 tablespoons butter |
| ½ teaspoon cumin | 2 tablespoons flour |
| ½ teaspoon onion powder | 235 ml chicken broth |
| ¼ teaspoon garlic powder | 60 g light sour cream |
| Salt and pepper, to taste | ¼ teaspoon salt |
| 8 flour tortillas (6- or 7-inch diameter) | 60 g Pepper Jack or Monterey Jack cheese, shredded |

1. Make the sauce by melting butter in a saucepan over medium-low heat. Stir in flour until smooth and slightly bubbly. Gradually add broth, stirring constantly until smooth. Cook and stir 1 minute, until the mixture slightly thickens. Remove from heat and stir in sour cream and salt. Set aside. 2. In a medium bowl, mix together the chicken, chilies, oregano, cumin, onion powder, garlic, salt, and pepper. Stir in 3 to 4 tablespoons of the sauce, using just enough to make the filling moist but not soupy. 3. Divide filling among the 8 tortillas. Place filling down the centre of tortilla, stopping about 1 inch from edges. Fold one side of tortilla over filling, fold the two sides in, and then roll up. Mist all sides with oil or cooking spray. 4. Place chimichangas in air fryer basket seam side down. To fit more into the basket, you can stand them on their sides with the seams against the sides of the basket. 5. Air fry at 180°C for 8 to 10 minutes or until heated through and crispy brown outside. 6. Add the shredded cheese to the remaining sauce. Stir over low heat, warming just until the cheese melts. Don't boil or sour cream may curdle. 7. Drizzle the sauce over the chimichangas.

## Fried Chicken Breasts

**Prep time: 30 minutes | Cook time: 12 to 14 minutes | Serves 4**

| | |
|---|---|
| 450 g boneless, skinless chicken breasts | cheese |
| 180 ml dill pickle juice | ½ teaspoon sea salt |
| 35 g finely ground blanched almond flour | ½ teaspoon freshly ground black pepper |
| 70 g finely grated Parmesan | 2 large eggs |
| | Avocado oil spray |

1. Place the chicken breasts in a zip-top bag or between two pieces of plastic wrap. Using a meat mallet or heavy skillet, pound the chicken to a uniform ½-inch thickness. 2. Place the chicken in a large bowl with the pickle juice. Cover and allow to brine in the refrigerator for up to 2 hours. 3. In a shallow dish, combine the almond flour, Parmesan cheese, salt, and pepper. In a separate, shallow bowl, beat the eggs. 4. Drain the chicken and pat it dry with paper towels. Dip in the eggs and then in the flour mixture, making sure to press the coating into the chicken. Spray both sides of the coated breasts with oil. 5. Spray the air fryer basket with oil and put the chicken inside. Set the temperature to 200ºC and air fry for 6 to 7 minutes. 6. Carefully flip the breasts with a spatula. Spray the breasts again with oil and continue cooking for 6 to 7 minutes more, until golden and crispy.

## Sweet Chili Spiced Chicken

**Prep time: 10 minutes | Cook time: 43 minutes | Serves 4**

| | |
|---|---|
| Spice Rub: | or kosher salt |
| 2 tablespoons brown sugar | 2 teaspoons coarsely ground black pepper |
| 2 tablespoons paprika | |
| 1 teaspoon dry mustard powder | 1 tablespoon vegetable oil |
| 1 teaspoon chili powder | 1 (1.6 kg) chicken, cut into 8 pieces |
| 2 tablespoons coarse sea salt | |

1. Prepare the spice rub by combining the brown sugar, paprika, mustard powder, chili powder, salt and pepper. Rub the oil all over the chicken pieces and then rub the spice mix onto the chicken, covering completely. This is done very easily in a zipper sealable bag. You can do this ahead of time and let the chicken marinate in the refrigerator, or just proceed with cooking right away. 2. Preheat the air fryer to 190ºC. 3. Air fry the chicken in two batches. Place the two chicken thighs and two drumsticks into the air fryer basket. Air fry at 190ºC for 10 minutes. Then, gently turn the chicken pieces over and air fry for another 10 minutes. Remove the chicken pieces and let them rest on a plate while you cook the chicken breasts. Air fry the chicken breasts, skin side down for 8 minutes. Turn the chicken breasts over and air fry for another 12 minutes. 4. Lower the temperature of the air fryer to 170ºC. Place the first batch of chicken on top of the second batch already in the basket and air fry for a final 3 minutes. 5. Let the chicken rest for 5 minutes and serve warm with some mashed potatoes and a green salad or vegetables.

## Cranberry Curry Chicken

**Prep time: 12 minutes | Cook time: 18 minutes | Serves 4**

| | |
|---|---|
| 3 (140 g) low-sodium boneless, skinless chicken breasts, cut into 1½-inch cubes | 1 tart apple, chopped |
| | 120 ml low-sodium chicken broth |
| 2 teaspoons olive oil | 60 g dried cranberries |
| 2 tablespoons cornflour | 2 tablespoons freshly squeezed orange juice |
| 1 tablespoon curry powder | Brown rice, cooked (optional) |

1. Preheat the air fryer to 196ºC. 2. In a medium bowl, mix the chicken and olive oil. Sprinkle with the cornflour and curry powder. Toss to coat. Stir in the apple and transfer to a metal pan. Bake in the air fryer for 8 minutes, stirring once during cooking. 3. Add the chicken broth, cranberries, and orange juice. Bake for about 10 minutes more, or until the sauce is slightly thickened and the chicken reaches an internal temperature of 76ºC on a meat thermometer. Serve over hot cooked brown rice, if desired.

## Classic Whole Chicken

**Prep time: 5 minutes | Cook time: 50 minutes | Serves 4**

| | |
|---|---|
| Oil, for spraying | ½ teaspoon salt |
| 1 (1.8 kg) whole chicken, giblets removed | ½ teaspoon freshly ground black pepper |
| 1 tablespoon olive oil | ¼ teaspoon finely chopped fresh parsley, for garnish |
| 1 teaspoon paprika | |
| ½ teaspoon granulated garlic | |

1. Line the air fryer basket with parchment and spray lightly with oil. 2. Pat the chicken dry with paper towels. Rub it with the olive oil until evenly coated. 3. In a small bowl, mix together the paprika, garlic, salt, and black pepper and sprinkle it evenly over the chicken. 4. Place the chicken in the prepared basket, breast-side down. 5. Air fry at 180ºC for 30 minutes, flip, and cook for another 20 minutes, or until the internal temperature reaches 76ºC and the juices run clear. 6. Sprinkle with the parsley before serving.

## Sweet and Spicy Turkey Meatballs

**Prep time: 15 minutes | Cook time: 15 minutes | Serves 6**

| | |
|---|---|
| Olive oil | sauce, divided |
| 450 g lean turkey mince | 2 teaspoons minced garlic |
| 30 g whole-wheat panko bread crumbs | ⅛ teaspoon salt |
| 1 egg, beaten | ⅛ teaspoon freshly ground black pepper |
| 1 tablespoon soy sauce | 1 teaspoon Sriracha |
| 60 ml plus 1 tablespoon hoisin | |

1. Spray the air fryer basket lightly with olive oil. 2. In a large bowl, mix together the turkey, panko bread crumbs, egg, soy sauce, 1 tablespoon of hoisin sauce, garlic, salt, and black pepper. 3. Using a tablespoon, form 24 meatballs. 4. In a small bowl, combine the remaining 60 ml of hoisin sauce and Sriracha to make a glaze and set aside. 5. Place the meatballs in the air fryer basket in a single layer. You may need to cook them in batches. 6. Air fry at 180°C for 8 minutes. Brush the meatballs generously with the glaze and cook until cooked through, an additional 4 to 7 minutes.

## Chicken and Ham Meatballs with Dijon Sauce

**Prep time: 10 minutes | Cook time: 15 minutes | Serves 4**

| | |
|---|---|
| Meatballs: | Cooking spray |
| 230 g ham, diced | Dijon Sauce: |
| 230 g chicken mince | 3 tablespoons Dijon mustard |
| 110 g grated Swiss cheese | 2 tablespoons lemon juice |
| 1 large egg, beaten | 60 ml chicken broth, warmed |
| 3 cloves garlic, minced | ¾ teaspoon sea salt |
| 15 g chopped onions | ¼ teaspoon ground black pepper |
| 1½ teaspoons sea salt | |
| 1 teaspoon ground black pepper | Chopped fresh thyme leaves, for garnish |

1. Preheat the air fryer to 200°C. Spritz the air fryer basket with cooking spray. 2. Combine the ingredients for the meatballs in a large bowl. Stir to mix well, then shape the mixture in twelve 1½-inch meatballs. 3. Arrange the meatballs in a single layer in the air fryer basket. Air fry for 15 minutes or until lightly browned. Flip the balls halfway through. You may need to work in batches to avoid overcrowding. 4. Meanwhile, combine the ingredients, except for the thyme leaves, for the sauce in a small bowl. Stir to mix well. 5. Transfer the cooked meatballs on a large plate, then baste the sauce over. Garnish with thyme leaves and serve.

## Spanish Chicken and Mini Sweet Pepper Baguette

**Prep time: 10 minutes | Cook time: 20 minutes | Serves 2**

| | |
|---|---|
| 570 g assorted small chicken parts, breasts cut into halves | 230 g mini sweet peppers |
| ¼ teaspoon salt | 60 g light mayonnaise |
| ¼ teaspoon ground black pepper | ¼ teaspoon smoked paprika |
| 2 teaspoons olive oil | ½ clove garlic, crushed |
| | Baguette, for serving |
| | Cooking spray |

1. Preheat air fryer to 190°C. Spritz the air fryer basket with cooking spray. 2. Toss the chicken with salt, ground black pepper, and olive oil in a large bowl. 3. Arrange the sweet peppers and chicken in the preheated air fryer and air fry for 10 minutes, then transfer the peppers on a plate. 4. Flip the chicken and air fry for 10 more minutes or until well browned. 5. Meanwhile, combine the mayo, paprika, and garlic in a small bowl. Stir to mix well. 6. Assemble the baguette with chicken and sweet pepper, then spread with mayo mixture and serve.

## Fiesta Chicken Plate

**Prep time: 15 minutes | Cook time: 12 to 15 minutes | Serves 4**

| | |
|---|---|
| 450 g boneless, skinless chicken breasts (2 large breasts) | 130 g salsa |
| | 30 g shredded lettuce |
| 2 tablespoons lime juice | 1 medium tomato, chopped |
| 1 teaspoon cumin | 2 avocados, peeled and sliced |
| ½ teaspoon salt | 1 small onion, sliced into thin rings |
| 40 g grated Pepper Jack cheese | Sour cream |
| 1 (455 g) can refried beans | Tortilla chips (optional) |

1. Split each chicken breast in half lengthwise. 2. Mix lime juice, cumin, and salt together and brush on all surfaces of chicken breasts. 3. Place in air fryer basket and air fry at 200°C for 12 to 15 minutes, until well done. 4. Divide the cheese evenly over chicken breasts and cook for an additional minute to melt cheese. 5. While chicken is cooking, heat refried beans on stovetop or in microwave. 6. When ready to serve, divide beans among 4 plates. Place chicken breasts on top of beans and spoon salsa over. Arrange the lettuce, tomatoes, and avocados artfully on each plate and scatter with the onion rings. 7. Pass sour cream at the table and serve with tortilla chips if desired.

## Chicken Drumsticks with Barbecue-Honey Sauce

**Prep time: 5 minutes | Cook time: 40 minutes | Serves 5**

| 1 tablespoon olive oil | Salt and ground black pepper, to taste |
| 10 chicken drumsticks | 240 ml barbecue sauce |
| Chicken seasoning or rub, to taste | 85 g honey |

1. Preheat the air fryer to 200ºC. Grease the air fryer basket with olive oil. 2. Rub the chicken drumsticks with chicken seasoning or rub, salt and ground black pepper on a clean work surface. 3. Arrange the chicken drumsticks in a single layer in the air fryer, then air fry for 18 minutes or until lightly browned. Flip the drumsticks halfway through. You may need to work in batches to avoid overcrowding. 4. Meanwhile, combine the barbecue sauce and honey in a small bowl. Stir to mix well. 5. Remove the drumsticks from the air fryer and baste with the sauce mixture to serve.

## Hawaiian Huli Huli Chicken

**Prep time: 30 minutes | Cook time: 15 minutes | Serves 4**

| 4 boneless, skinless chicken thighs (680 g) | 25 g sugar |
| 1 (230 g) can pineapple chunks in juice, drained, 60 ml juice reserved | 2 tablespoons ketchup |
| | 1 tablespoon minced fresh ginger |
| 60 ml soy sauce | 1 tablespoon minced garlic |
| | 25 g chopped spring onions |

1. Use a fork to pierce the chicken all over to allow the marinade to penetrate better. Place the chicken in a large bowl or large resealable plastic bag. 2. Set the drained pineapple chunks aside. In a small microwave-safe bowl, combine the pineapple juice, soy sauce, sugar, ketchup, ginger, and garlic. Pour half the sauce over the chicken; toss to coat. Reserve the remaining sauce. Marinate the chicken at room temperature for 30 minutes, or cover and refrigerate for up to 24 hours. 3. Place the chicken in the air fryer basket. (Discard marinade.) Set the air fryer to 180ºC for 15 minutes, turning halfway through the cooking time. 4. Meanwhile, microwave the reserved sauce on high for 45 to 60 seconds, stirring every 15 seconds, until the sauce has the consistency of a thick glaze. 5. At the end of the cooking time, use a meat thermometer to ensure the chicken has reached an internal temperature of 76ºC. 6. Transfer the chicken to a serving platter. Pour the sauce over the chicken. Garnish with the pineapple chunks and spring onions.

## Bruschetta Chicken

**Prep time: 10 minutes | Cook time: 20 minutes | Serves 4**

| Bruschetta Stuffing: | olive oil |
| 1 tomato, diced | Chicken: |
| 3 tablespoons balsamic vinegar | 4 (115 g) boneless, skinless chicken breasts, cut 4 slits each |
| 1 teaspoon Italian seasoning | 1 teaspoon Italian seasoning |
| 2 tablespoons chopped fresh basil | Chicken seasoning or rub, to taste |
| 3 garlic cloves, minced | Cooking spray |
| 2 tablespoons extra-virgin | |

1. Preheat the air fryer to 190º. Spritz the air fryer basket with cooking spray. 2. Combine the ingredients for the bruschetta stuffing in a bowl. Stir to mix well. Set aside. 3. Rub the chicken breasts with Italian seasoning and chicken seasoning on a clean work surface. 4. Arrange the chicken breasts, slits side up, in a single layer in the air fryer basket and spritz with cooking spray. You may need to work in batches to avoid overcrowding. 5. Air fry for 7 minutes, then open the air fryer and fill the slits in the chicken with the bruschetta stuffing. Cook for another 3 minutes or until the chicken is well browned. 6. Serve immediately.

## Crispy Dill Chicken Strips

**Prep time: 30 minutes | Cook time: 10 minutes | Serves 4**

| 2 whole boneless, skinless chicken breasts (about 450 g each), halved lengthwise | 1 tablespoon dried dill weed |
| | 1 tablespoon garlic powder |
| | 1 large egg, beaten |
| 230 ml Italian dressing | 1 to 2 tablespoons oil |
| 110 g finely crushed crisps | |

1. In a large resealable bag, combine the chicken and Italian dressing. Seal the bag and refrigerate to marinate at least 1 hour. 2. In a shallow dish, stir together the potato chips, dill, and garlic powder. Place the beaten egg in a second shallow dish. 3. Remove the chicken from the marinade. Roll the chicken pieces in the egg and the crisp mixture, coating thoroughly. 4. Preheat the air fryer to 170ºC. Line the air fryer basket with parchment paper. 5. Place the coated chicken on the parchment and spritz with oil. 6. Cook for 5 minutes. Flip the chicken, spritz it with oil, and cook for 5 minutes more until the outsides are crispy and the insides are no longer pink.

## Bacon-Wrapped Chicken Breasts Rolls

**Prep time: 10 minutes | Cook time: 15 minutes | Serves 4**

| | |
|---|---|
| 15 g chopped fresh chives | ½ teaspoon red pepper flakes |
| 2 tablespoons lemon juice | 4 (115 g) boneless, skinless chicken breasts, pounded to ¼ inch thick |
| 1 teaspoon dried sage | |
| 1 teaspoon fresh rosemary leaves | 8 slices bacon |
| 15 g fresh parsley leaves | Sprigs of fresh rosemary, for garnish |
| 4 cloves garlic, peeled | |
| 1 teaspoon ground fennel | Cooking spray |
| 3 teaspoons sea salt | |

1. Preheat the air fryer to 170°C. Spritz the air fryer basket with cooking spray. 2. Put the chives, lemon juice, sage, rosemary, parsley, garlic, fennel, salt, and red pepper flakes in a food processor, then pulse to purée until smooth. 3. Unfold the chicken breasts on a clean work surface, then brush the top side of the chicken breasts with the sauce. 4. Roll the chicken breasts up from the shorter side, then wrap each chicken rolls with 2 bacon slices to cover. Secure with toothpicks. 5. Arrange the rolls in the preheated air fryer, then cook for 10 minutes. Flip the rolls halfway through. 6. Increase the heat to 200°C and air fry for 5 more minutes or until the bacon is browned and crispy. 7. Transfer the rolls to a large plate. Discard the toothpicks and spread with rosemary sprigs before serving.

## Wild Rice and Kale Stuffed Chicken Thighs

**Prep time: 10 minutes | Cook time: 22 minutes | Serves 4**

| | |
|---|---|
| 4 boneless, skinless chicken thighs | 1 teaspoon salt |
| | Juice of 1 lemon |
| 250 g cooked wild rice | 100 g crumbled feta |
| 35 g chopped kale | Olive oil cooking spray |
| 2 garlic cloves, minced | 1 tablespoon olive oi |

1. Preheat the air fryer to 192°C. 2. Place the chicken thighs between two pieces of plastic wrap, and using a meat mallet or a rolling pin, pound them out to about ¼-inch thick. 3. In a medium bowl, combine the rice, kale, garlic, salt, and lemon juice and mix well. 4. Place a quarter of the rice mixture into the middle of each chicken thigh, then sprinkle 2 tablespoons of feta over the filling. 5. Spray the air fryer basket with olive oil cooking spray. 6. Fold the sides of the chicken thigh over the filling, and then gently place each of them seam-side down into the air fryer basket. Brush each stuffed chicken thigh with olive oil. 7. Roast the stuffed chicken thighs for 12 minutes, then turn them over and cook for an additional 10 minutes, or until the internal temperature reaches 76°C.

## Easy Chicken Fingers

**Prep time: 20 minutes | Cook time: 30 minutes | Makes 12 chicken fingers**

| | |
|---|---|
| 30 g all-purpose flour | chicken breasts, each cut into 4 strips |
| 120 g panko breadcrumbs | |
| 2 tablespoons rapeseed oil | Kosher salt and freshly ground black pepper, to taste |
| 1 large egg | |
| 3 boneless and skinless | Cooking spray |

1. Preheat the air fryer to 180°C. Spritz the air fryer basket with cooking spray. 2. Pour the flour in a large bowl. Combine the panko and rapeseed oil on a shallow dish. Whisk the egg in a separate bowl. 3. Rub the chicken strips with salt and ground black pepper on a clean work surface, then dip the chicken in the bowl of flour. Shake the excess off and dunk the chicken strips in the bowl of whisked egg, then roll the strips over the panko to coat well. 4. Arrange 4 strips in the air fryer basket each time and air fry for 10 minutes or until crunchy and lightly browned. Flip the strips halfway through. Repeat with remaining ingredients. 5. Serve immediately.

## Potato-Crusted Chicken

**Prep time: 15 minutes | Cook time: 22 to 25 minutes | Serves 4**

| | |
|---|---|
| 60 g buttermilk | black pepper |
| 1 large egg, beaten | 2 whole boneless, skinless chicken breasts (about 450 g each), halved |
| 180 g instant potato flakes | |
| 20 g grated Parmesan cheese | |
| 1 teaspoon salt | 1 to 2 tablespoons oil |
| ½ teaspoon freshly ground | |

1. In a shallow bowl, whisk the buttermilk and egg until blended. In another shallow bowl, stir together the potato flakes, cheese, salt, and pepper. 2. One at a time, dip the chicken pieces in the buttermilk mixture and the potato flake mixture, coating thoroughly. 3. Preheat the air fryer to 200°C. Line the air fryer basket with parchment paper. 4. Place the coated chicken on the parchment and spritz with oil. 5. Cook for 15 minutes. Flip the chicken, spritz it with oil, and cook for 7 to 10 minutes more until the outside is crispy and the inside is no longer pink.

# Gochujang Chicken Wings

**Prep time: 15 minutes | Cook time: 25 minutes | Serves 4**

| | |
|---|---|
| Wings: | oil |
| 900 g chicken wings | 1 tablespoon minced fresh ginger |
| 1 teaspoon kosher salt | 1 tablespoon minced garlic |
| 1 teaspoon black pepper or gochugaru (Korean red pepper) | 1 teaspoon sugar |
| | 1 teaspoon agave nectar or honey |
| Sauce: | For Serving |
| 2 tablespoons gochujang (Korean chili paste) | 1 teaspoon sesame seeds |
| 1 tablespoon mayonnaise | 25 g chopped spring onions |
| 1 tablespoon toasted sesame | |

1. For the wings: Season the wings with the salt and pepper and place in the air fryer basket. Set the air fryer to 200ºC for 20 minutes, turning the wings halfway through the cooking time. 2. Meanwhile, for the sauce: In a small bowl, combine the gochujang, mayonnaise, sesame oil, ginger, garlic, sugar, and agave; set aside. 3. As you near the 20-minute mark, use a meat thermometer to check the meat. When the wings reach 70ºC, transfer them to a large bowl. Pour about half the sauce on the wings; toss to coat (serve the remaining sauce as a dip). 4. Return the wings to the air fryer basket and cook for 5 minutes, until the sauce has glazed. 5. Transfer the wings to a serving platter. Sprinkle with the sesame seeds and spring onions. Serve with the reserved sauce on the side for dipping.

# Israeli Chicken Schnitzel

**Prep time: 5 minutes | Cook time: 10 minutes | Serves 4**

| | |
|---|---|
| 2 large boneless, skinless chicken breasts, each weighing about 450 g | 1 teaspoon paprika |
| | 2 eggs beaten with 2 tablespoons water |
| 65 g all-purpose flour | 125 g panko bread crumbs |
| 2 teaspoons garlic powder | Vegetable oil spray |
| 2 teaspoons kosher salt | Lemon juice, for serving |
| 1 teaspoon black pepper | |

1. Preheat the air fryer to 190ºC. 2. Place 1 chicken breast between 2 pieces of plastic wrap. Use a mallet or a rolling pin to pound the chicken until it is ¼ inch thick. Set aside. Repeat with the second breast. Whisk together the flour, garlic powder, salt, pepper, and paprika on a large plate. Place the panko in a separate shallow bowl or pie plate. 3. Dredge 1 chicken breast in the flour, shaking off any excess, then dip it in the egg mixture. Dredge the chicken breast in the panko, making sure to coat it completely. Shake off any excess panko. Place the battered chicken breast on a plate. Repeat with the second chicken breast. 4. Spray the air fryer basket with oil spray. Place 1 of the battered chicken breasts in the basket and spray the top with oil spray. Air fry until the top is browned, about 5 minutes. Flip the chicken and spray the second side with oil spray. Air fry until the second side is browned and crispy and the internal temperature reaches 76ºC. Remove the first chicken breast from the air fryer and repeat with the second chicken breast. 5. Serve hot with lemon juice.

# Crispy Duck with Cherry Sauce

**Prep time: 10 minutes | Cook time: 33 minutes | Serves 2 to 4**

| | |
|---|---|
| 1 whole duck (2.3 kg), split in half, back and rib bones removed | 1 shallot, minced |
| | 120 ml sherry |
| | 240 g cherry preserves |
| 1 teaspoon olive oil | 240 ml chicken stock |
| Salt and freshly ground black pepper, to taste | 1 teaspoon white wine vinegar |
| | 1 teaspoon fresh thyme leaves |
| Cherry Sauce: | Salt and freshly ground black pepper, to taste |
| 1 tablespoon butter | |

1. Preheat the air fryer to 200ºC. 2. Trim some of the fat from the duck. Rub olive oil on the duck and season with salt and pepper. Place the duck halves in the air fryer basket, breast side up and facing the centre of the basket. 3. Air fry the duck for 20 minutes. Turn the duck over and air fry for another 6 minutes. 4. While duck is air frying, make the cherry sauce. Melt the butter in a large sauté pan. Add the shallot and sauté until it is just starting to brown, about 2 to 3 minutes. Add the sherry and deglaze the pan by scraping up any brown bits from the bottom of the pan. Simmer the liquid for a few minutes, until it has reduced by half. Add the cherry preserves, chicken stock and white wine vinegar. Whisk well to combine all the ingredients. Simmer the sauce until it thickens and coats the back of a spoon, about 5 to 7 minutes. Season with salt and pepper and stir in the fresh thyme leaves. 5. When the air fryer timer goes off, spoon some cherry sauce over the duck and continue to air fry at 200ºC for 4 more minutes. Then, turn the duck halves back over so that the breast side is facing up. Spoon more cherry sauce over the top of the duck, covering the skin completely. Air fry for 3 more minutes and then remove the duck to a plate to rest for a few minutes. 6. Serve the duck in halves, or cut each piece in half again for a smaller serving. Spoon any additional sauce over the duck or serve it on the side.

## Ham Chicken with Cheese

**Prep time: 15 minutes | Cook time: 25 minutes | Serves 4**

| | |
|---|---|
| 55 g unsalted butter, softened | 280 g shredded cooked chicken |
| 115 g cream cheese, softened | 115 g ham, chopped |
| 1½ teaspoons Dijon mustard | 115 g sliced Swiss or Provolone cheese |
| 2 tablespoons white wine vinegar | |
| 60 ml water | |

1. Preheat the air fryer to 190°C. Lightly coat a casserole dish that will fit in the air fryer, such as an 8-inch round pan, with olive oil and set aside. 2. In a large bowl and using an electric mixer, combine the butter, cream cheese, Dijon mustard, and vinegar. With the motor running at low speed, slowly add the water and beat until smooth. Set aside. 3. Arrange an even layer of chicken in the bottom of the prepared pan, followed by the ham. Spread the butter and cream cheese mixture on top of the ham, followed by the cheese slices on the top layer. Air fry for 20 to 25 minutes until warmed through and the cheese has browned.

## Herb-Buttermilk Chicken Breast

**Prep time: 5 minutes | Cook time: 40 minutes | Serves 2**

| | |
|---|---|
| 1 large bone-in, skin-on chicken breast | ½ teaspoon dried dill |
| 240 ml buttermilk | ½ teaspoon onion powder |
| 1½ teaspoons dried parsley | ¼ teaspoon garlic powder |
| 1½ teaspoons dried chives | ¼ teaspoon dried tarragon |
| ¾ teaspoon kosher salt | Cooking spray |

1. Place the chicken breast in a bowl and pour over the buttermilk, turning the chicken in it to make sure it's completely covered. Let the chicken stand at room temperature for at least 20 minutes or in the refrigerator for up to 4 hours. 2. Meanwhile, in a bowl, stir together the parsley, chives, salt, dill, onion powder, garlic powder, and tarragon. 3. Preheat the air fryer to 150°C. 4. Remove the chicken from the buttermilk, letting the excess drip off, then place the chicken skin-side up directly in the air fryer. Sprinkle the seasoning mix all over the top of the chicken breast, then let stand until the herb mix soaks into the buttermilk, at least 5 minutes. 5. Spray the top of the chicken with cooking spray. Bake for 10 minutes, then increase the temperature to 180°C and bake until an instant-read thermometer inserted into the thickest part of the breast reads 80°C and the chicken is deep golden brown, 30 to 35 minutes. 6. Transfer the chicken breast to a cutting board, let rest for 10 minutes, then cut the meat off the bone and cut into thick slices for serving.

## Chicken Jalfrezi

**Prep time: 15 minutes | Cook time: 15 minutes | Serves 4**

| | |
|---|---|
| Chicken: | 1 teaspoon kosher salt |
| 450 g boneless, skinless chicken thighs, cut into 2 or 3 pieces each | ½ to 1 teaspoon cayenne pepper |
| | Sauce: |
| 1 medium onion, chopped | 55 g tomato sauce |
| 1 large green bell pepper, stemmed, seeded, and chopped | 1 tablespoon water |
| | 1 teaspoon garam masala |
| | ½ teaspoon kosher salt |
| 2 tablespoons olive oil | ½ teaspoon cayenne pepper |
| 1 teaspoon ground turmeric | Side salad, rice, or naan bread, for serving |
| 1 teaspoon garam masala | |

1. For the chicken: In a large bowl, combine the chicken, onion, bell pepper, oil, turmeric, garam masala, salt, and cayenne. Stir and toss until well combined. 2. Place the chicken and vegetables in the air fryer basket. Set the air fryer to 180°C for 15 minutes, stirring and tossing halfway through the cooking time. Use a meat thermometer to ensure the chicken has reached an internal temperature of 76°C. 3. Meanwhile, for the sauce: In a small microwave-safe bowl, combine the tomato sauce, water, garam masala, salt, and cayenne. Microwave on high for 1 minute. Remove and stir. Microwave for another minute; set aside. 4. When the chicken is cooked, remove and place chicken and vegetables in a large bowl. Pour the sauce over all. Stir and toss to coat the chicken and vegetables evenly. 5. Serve with rice, naan, or a side salad.

# Chapter 5
# Vegetables and Sides

# Chapter 5 Vegetables and Sides

## Crispy Garlic Sliced Aubergine

**Prep time: 5 minutes | Cook time: 25 minutes | Serves 4**

| | |
|---|---|
| 1 egg | ½ teaspoon salt |
| 1 tablespoon water | ½ teaspoon paprika |
| 60 g whole wheat bread crumbs | 1 medium aubergine, sliced into ¼-inch-thick rounds |
| 1 teaspoon garlic powder | 1 tablespoon olive oil |
| ½ teaspoon dried oregano | |

1. Preheat the air fryer to 180°C. 2. In a medium shallow bowl, beat together the egg and water until frothy. 3. In a separate medium shallow bowl, mix together bread crumbs, garlic powder, oregano, salt, and paprika. 4. Dip each aubergine slice into the egg mixture, then into the bread crumb mixture, coating the outside with crumbs. Place the slices in a single layer in the bottom of the air fryer basket. 5. Drizzle the tops of the aubergine slices with the olive oil, then fry for 15 minutes. Turn each slice and cook for an additional 10 minutes.

## Polenta Casserole

**Prep time: 5 minutes | Cook time: 28 to 30 minutes | Serves 4**

| | |
|---|---|
| 10 fresh asparagus spears, cut into 1-inch pieces | ½ teaspoon garlic powder |
| 320 g cooked polenta, cooled to room temperature | ¼ teaspoon salt |
| | 2 slices emmental cheese (about 40 g) |
| 1 egg, beaten | Oil for misting or cooking spray |
| 2 teaspoons Worcestershire sauce | |

1. Mist asparagus spears with oil and air fry at 200°C for 5 minutes, until crisp-tender. 2. In a medium bowl, mix together the grits, egg, Worcestershire, garlic powder, and salt. 3. Spoon half of polenta mixture into a baking pan and top with asparagus. 4. Tear cheese slices into pieces and layer evenly on top of asparagus. 5. Top with remaining polenta. 6. Bake at 180°C for 23 to 25 minutes. The casserole will rise a little as it cooks. When done, the top will have browned lightly with just a hint of crispiness.

## Cauliflower Steaks Gratin

**Prep time: 10 minutes | Cook time: 13 minutes | Serves 2**

| | |
|---|---|
| 1 head cauliflower | thyme leaves |
| 1 tablespoon olive oil | 3 tablespoons grated Parmigiano-Reggiano cheese |
| Salt and freshly ground black pepper, to taste | 2 tablespoons panko bread crumbs |
| ½ teaspoon chopped fresh | |

1. Preheat the air fryer to 190°C. 2. Cut two steaks out of the centre of the cauliflower. To do this, cut the cauliflower in half and then cut one slice about 1-inch thick off each half. The rest of the cauliflower will fall apart into florets, which you can roast on their own or save for another meal. 3. Brush both sides of the cauliflower steaks with olive oil and season with salt, freshly ground black pepper and fresh thyme. Place the cauliflower steaks into the air fryer basket and air fry for 6 minutes. Turn the steaks over and air fry for another 4 minutes. Combine the Parmesan cheese and panko bread crumbs and sprinkle the mixture over the tops of both steaks and air fry for another 3 minutes until the cheese has melted and the bread crumbs have browned. Serve this with some sautéed bitter greens and air-fried blistered tomatoes.

## Roasted Brussels Sprouts with Bacon

**Prep time: 10 minutes | Cook time: 20 minutes | Serves 4**

| | |
|---|---|
| 4 slices thick-cut bacon, chopped (about 110 g) | (or quartered if large) |
| | Freshly ground black pepper, to taste |
| 450 g Brussels sprouts, halved | |

1. Preheat the air fryer to 190°C. 2. Air fry the bacon for 5 minutes, shaking the basket once or twice during the cooking time. 3. Add the Brussels sprouts to the basket and drizzle a little bacon fat from the bottom of the air fryer drawer into the basket. Toss the sprouts to coat with the bacon fat. Air fry for an additional 15 minutes, or until the Brussels sprouts are tender to a knifepoint. 4. Season with freshly ground black pepper.

## Cauliflower with Lime Juice

**Prep time: 10 minutes | Cook time: 7 minutes | Serves 4**

- 215 g chopped cauliflower florets
- 2 tablespoons coconut oil, melted
- 2 teaspoons chili powder
- ½ teaspoon garlic powder
- 1 medium lime
- 2 tablespoons chopped coriander

1. In a large bowl, toss cauliflower with coconut oil. Sprinkle with chili powder and garlic powder. Place seasoned cauliflower into the air fryer basket. 2. Adjust the temperature to 180°C and set the timer for 7 minutes. 3. Cauliflower will be tender and begin to turn golden at the edges. Place into a serving bowl. 4. Cut the lime into quarters and squeeze juice over cauliflower. Garnish with coriander.

## Flatbread

**Prep time: 5 minutes | Cook time: 7 minutes | Serves 2**

- 225 g shredded Mozzarella cheese
- 25 g blanched finely ground almond flour
- 30 g full-fat cream cheese, softened

1. In a large microwave-safe bowl, melt Mozzarella in the microwave for 30 seconds. Stir in almond flour until smooth and then add cream cheese. Continue mixing until dough forms, gently kneading it with wet hands if necessary. 2. Divide the dough into two pieces and roll out to ¼-inch thickness between two pieces of parchment. Cut another piece of parchment to fit your air fryer basket. 3. Place a piece of flatbread onto your parchment and into the air fryer, working in two batches if needed. 4. Adjust the temperature to 160°C and air fry for 7 minutes. 5. Halfway through the cooking time flip the flatbread. Serve warm.

## Indian Aubergine Bharta

**Prep time: 15 minutes | Cook time: 20 minutes | Serves 4**

- 1 medium aubergine
- 2 tablespoons vegetable oil
- 25 g finely minced onion
- 100 g finely chopped fresh tomato
- 2 tablespoons fresh lemon juice
- 2 tablespoons chopped fresh coriander
- ½ teaspoon coarse sea salt
- ⅛ teaspoon cayenne pepper

1. Rub the aubergine all over with the vegetable oil. Place the aubergine in the air fryer basket. Set the air fryer to 200°C for 20 minutes, or until the aubergine skin is blistered and charred. 2. Transfer the aubergine to a re-sealable plastic bag, seal, and set aside for 15 to 20 minutes (the aubergine will finish cooking in the residual heat trapped in the bag). 3. Transfer the aubergine to a large bowl. Peel off and discard the charred skin. Roughly mash the aubergine flesh. Add the onion, tomato, lemon juice, coriander, salt, and cayenne. Stir to combine.

## Mexican Corn in a Cup

**Prep time: 5 minutes | Cook time: 10 minutes | Serves 4**

- 650 g frozen corn kernels (do not thaw)
- Vegetable oil spray
- 2 tablespoons butter
- 60 g sour cream
- 60 g mayonnaise
- 20 g grated Parmesan cheese (or feta, cotija, or queso fresco)
- 2 tablespoons fresh lemon or lime juice
- 1 teaspoon chili powder
- Chopped fresh green onion (optional)
- Chopped fresh coriander (optional)

1. Place the corn in the bottom of the air fryer basket and spray with vegetable oil spray. Set the air fryer to 180°C for 10 minutes. 2. Transfer the corn to a serving bowl. Add the butter and stir until melted. Add the sour cream, mayonnaise, cheese, lemon juice, and chili powder; stir until well combined. Serve immediately with green onion and coriander (if using).

## Cheese-Walnut Stuffed Mushrooms

**Prep time: 5 minutes | Cook time: 10 minutes | Serves 4**

- 4 large portobello mushrooms
- 1 tablespoon rapeseed oil
- 110 g shredded Mozzarella cheese
- 35 g minced walnuts
- 2 tablespoons chopped fresh parsley
- Cooking spray

1. Preheat the air fryer to 180°C. Spritz the air fryer basket with cooking spray. 2. On a clean work surface, remove the mushroom stems. Scoop out the gills with a spoon and discard. Coat the mushrooms with rapeseed oil. Top each mushroom evenly with the shredded Mozzarella cheese, followed by the minced walnuts. 3. Arrange the mushrooms in the air fryer and roast for 10 minutes until golden brown. 4. Transfer the mushrooms to a plate and sprinkle the parsley on top for garnish before serving.

## Sweet-and-Sour Brussels Sprouts

**Prep time: 10 minutes | Cook time: 20 minutes | Serves 2**

| | |
|---|---|
| 70 g Thai sweet chili sauce | 2 small shallots, cut into |
| 2 tablespoons black vinegar or balsamic vinegar | ¼-inch-thick slices |
| ½ teaspoon hot sauce, such as Tabasco | coarse sea salt and freshly ground black pepper, to taste |
| 230 g Brussels sprouts, trimmed (large sprouts halved) | 2 teaspoons lightly packed fresh coriander leaves |

1. In a large bowl, whisk together the chili sauce, vinegar, and hot sauce. Add the Brussels sprouts and shallots, season with salt and pepper, and toss to combine. Scrape the Brussels sprouts and sauce into a cake pan. 2. Place the pan in the air fryer and roast at 190ºC, stirring every 5 minutes, until the Brussels sprouts are tender and the sauce is reduced to a sticky glaze, about 20 minutes. 3. Remove the pan from the air fryer and transfer the Brussels sprouts to plates. Sprinkle with the coriander and serve warm.

## Roasted Aubergine

**Prep time: 15 minutes | Cook time: 15 minutes | Serves 4**

| | |
|---|---|
| 1 large aubergine | ¼ teaspoon salt |
| 2 tablespoons olive oil | ½ teaspoon garlic powder |

1. Remove top and bottom from aubergine. Slice aubergine into ¼-inch-thick round slices. 2. Brush slices with olive oil. Sprinkle with salt and garlic powder. Place aubergine slices into the air fryer basket. 3. Adjust the temperature to 200ºC and set the timer for 15 minutes. 4. Serve immediately.

## Parmesan-Rosemary Radishes

**Prep time: 5 minutes | Cook time: 15 to 20 minutes | Serves 4**

| | |
|---|---|
| 1 bunch radishes, stemmed, trimmed, and quartered | 1 tablespoon chopped fresh rosemary |
| 1 tablespoon avocado oil | Sea salt and freshly ground black pepper, to taste |
| 2 tablespoons finely grated fresh Parmesan cheese | |

1. Place the radishes in a medium bowl and toss them with the avocado oil, Parmesan cheese, rosemary, salt, and pepper. 2. Set the air fryer to 190ºC. Arrange the radishes in a single layer in the air fryer basket. Roast for 15 to 20 minutes, until golden brown and tender. Let cool for 5 minutes before serving.

## Breaded Green Tomatoes

**Prep time: 15 minutes | Cook time: 30 minutes | Serves 4**

| | |
|---|---|
| 60 g plain flour | Salt and freshly ground black pepper, to taste |
| 2 eggs | 2 green tomatoes, cut into |
| 60 g semolina | ½-inch-thick rounds |
| 60 g panko bread crumbs | Cooking oil spray |
| 1 teaspoon garlic powder | |

1. Place the flour in a small bowl. 2. In another small bowl, beat the eggs. 3. In a third small bowl, stir together the semolina, panko, and garlic powder. Season with salt and pepper. 4. Dip each tomato slice into the flour, the egg, and finally the semolina mixture to coat. 5. Insert the crisper plate into the basket and the basket into the unit. Preheat the unit by selecting AIR FRY, setting the temperature to 200ºC, and setting the time to 3 minutes. Select START/STOP to begin. 6. Once the unit is preheated, spray the crisper plate and the basket with cooking oil. Working in batches, place the tomato slices in the air fryer in a single layer. Do not stack them. Spray the tomato slices with the cooking oil. 7. Select AIR FRY, set the temperature to 200ºC, and set the time to 10 minutes. Select START/STOP to begin. 8. After 5 minutes, use tongs to flip the tomatoes. Resume cooking for 4 to 5 minutes, or until crisp. 9. When the cooking is complete, transfer the fried green tomatoes to a plate. Repeat steps 6, 7, and 8 for the remaining tomatoes.

## Tofu Bites

**Prep time: 15 minutes | Cook time: 30 minutes | Serves 4**

| | |
|---|---|
| 1 packaged firm tofu, cubed and pressed to remove excess water | 1 teaspoon liquid smoke |
| | 1 teaspoon hot sauce |
| | 2 tablespoons sesame seeds |
| 1 tablespoon soy sauce | 1 teaspoon garlic powder |
| 1 tablespoon ketchup | Salt and ground black pepper, to taste |
| 1 tablespoon maple syrup | Cooking spray |
| ½ teaspoon vinegar | |

1. Preheat the air fryer to 190ºC. 2. Spritz a baking dish with cooking spray. 3. Combine all the ingredients to coat the tofu completely and allow the marinade to absorb for half an hour. 4. Transfer the tofu to the baking dish, then air fry for 15 minutes. Flip the tofu over and air fry for another 15 minutes on the other side. 5. Serve immediately.

## Corn and Coriander Salad

**Prep time: 10 minutes | Cook time: 10 minutes | Serves 2**

| | |
|---|---|
| 2 ears of corn, shucked (halved crosswise if too large to fit in your air fryer) | coriander leaves |
| | 1 tablespoon sour cream |
| | 1 tablespoon mayonnaise |
| 1 tablespoon unsalted butter, at room temperature | 1 teaspoon adobo sauce (from a can of chipotle peppers in adobo sauce) |
| 1 teaspoon chili powder | |
| ¼ teaspoon garlic powder | 2 tablespoons crumbled feta cheese |
| coarse sea salt and freshly ground black pepper, to taste | |
| 20 g lightly packed fresh | Lime wedges, for serving |

1. Brush the corn all over with the butter, then sprinkle with the chili powder and garlic powder, and season with salt and pepper. Place the corn in the air fryer and air fry at 200°C, turning over halfway through, until the kernels are lightly charred and tender, about 10 minutes. 2. Transfer the ears to a cutting board, let stand 1 minute, then carefully cut the kernels off the cobs and move them to a bowl. Add the coriander leaves and toss to combine (the coriander leaves will wilt slightly). 3. In a small bowl, stir together the sour cream, mayonnaise, and adobo sauce. Divide the corn and coriander among plates and spoon the adobo dressing over the top. Sprinkle with the feta cheese and serve with lime wedges on the side.

## Mole-Braised Cauliflower

**Prep time: 10 minutes | Cook time: 15 minutes | Serves 2**

| | |
|---|---|
| 230 g medium cauliflower florets | peanuts |
| | 1 tablespoon toasted sesame seeds, plus more for garnish |
| 1 tablespoon vegetable oil | |
| coarse sea salt and freshly ground black pepper, to taste | 1 tablespoon finely chopped golden raisins |
| 350 ml vegetable stock | 1 teaspoon coarse sea salt |
| 2 tablespoons New Mexico chili powder (or regular chili powder) | 1 teaspoon dark brown sugar |
| | ½ teaspoon dried oregano |
| | ¼ teaspoon cayenne pepper |
| 2 tablespoons salted roasted | ⅛ teaspoon ground cinnamon |

1. In a large bowl, toss the cauliflower with the oil and season with salt and black pepper. Transfer to a cake pan. Place the pan in the air fryer and roast at 190°C until the cauliflower is tender and lightly browned at the edges, about 10 minutes, stirring halfway through. 2. Meanwhile, in a small blender, combine the stock, chili powder, peanuts, sesame seeds, raisins, salt, brown sugar, oregano, cayenne, and cinnamon and purée until smooth. Pour into a small saucepan or skillet and bring to a simmer over medium heat, then cook until reduced by half, 3 to 5 minutes. 3. Pour the hot mole sauce over the cauliflower in the pan, stir to coat, then cook until the sauce is thickened and lightly charred on the cauliflower, about 5 minutes more. Sprinkle with more sesame seeds and serve warm.

## Asparagus Fries

**Prep time: 15 minutes | Cook time: 5 to 7 minutes per batch | Serves 4**

| | |
|---|---|
| 340 g fresh asparagus spears with tough ends trimmed off | 25 g grated Parmesan cheese, plus 2 tablespoons |
| 2 egg whites | ¼ teaspoon salt |
| 60 ml water | Oil for misting or cooking spray |
| 80 g panko bread crumbs | |

1. Preheat the air fryer to 200°C. 2. In a shallow dish, beat egg whites and water until slightly foamy. 3. In another shallow dish, combine panko, Parmesan, and salt. 4. Dip asparagus spears in egg, then roll in crumbs. Spray with oil or cooking spray. 5. Place a layer of asparagus in air fryer basket, leaving just a little space in between each spear. Stack another layer on top, crosswise. Air fry at 200°C for 5 to 7 minutes, until crispy and golden brown. 6. Repeat to cook remaining asparagus.

## Brussels Sprouts with Pecans and Gorgonzola

**Prep time: 10 minutes | Cook time: 25 minutes | Serves 4**

| | |
|---|---|
| 65 g pecans | Salt and freshly ground black pepper, to taste |
| 680 g fresh Brussels sprouts, trimmed and quartered | |
| 2 tablespoons olive oil | 30 g crumbled Gorgonzola cheese |

1. Spread the pecans in a single layer of the air fryer and set the heat to 180°C. Air fry for 3 to 5 minutes until the pecans are lightly browned and fragrant. Transfer the pecans to a plate and continue preheating the air fryer, increasing the heat to 200°C. 2. In a large bowl, toss the Brussels sprouts with the olive oil and season with salt and black pepper to taste. 3. Working in batches if necessary, arrange the Brussels sprouts in a single layer in the air fryer basket. Pausing halfway through the baking time to shake the basket, air fry for 20 to 25 minutes until the sprouts are tender and starting to brown on the edges. 4. Transfer the sprouts to a serving bowl and top with the toasted pecans and Gorgonzola. Serve warm or at room temperature.

# Cabbage Wedges with Caraway Butter

**Prep time: 30 minutes | Cook time: 35 to 40 minutes | Serves 6**

- 1 tablespoon caraway seeds
- 110 g unsalted butter, at room temperature
- ½ teaspoon grated lemon zest
- 1 small head green or red cabbage, cut into 6 wedges
- 1 tablespoon avocado oil
- ½ teaspoon sea salt
- ¼ teaspoon freshly ground black pepper

1. Place the caraway seeds in a small dry skillet over medium-high heat. Toast the seeds for 2 to 3 minutes, then remove them from the heat and let cool. Lightly crush the seeds using a mortar and pestle or with the back of a knife. 2. Place the butter in a small bowl and stir in the crushed caraway seeds and lemon zest. Form the butter into a log and wrap it in parchment paper or plastic wrap. Refrigerate for at least 1 hour or freeze for 20 minutes. 3. Brush or spray the cabbage wedges with the avocado oil, and sprinkle with the salt and pepper. 4. Set the air fryer to 190°C. Place the cabbage in a single layer in the air fryer basket and roast for 20 minutes. Flip and cook for 15 to 20 minutes more, until the cabbage is tender and lightly charred. Plate the cabbage and dot with caraway butter. Tent with foil for 5 minutes to melt the butter, and serve.

# Caesar Whole Cauliflower

**Prep time: 20 minutes | Cook time: 30 minutes | Serves 2 to 4**

- 3 tablespoons olive oil
- 2 tablespoons red wine vinegar
- 2 tablespoons Worcestershire sauce
- 2 tablespoons grated Parmesan cheese
- 1 tablespoon Dijon mustard
- 4 garlic cloves, minced
- 4 oil-packed anchovy fillets, drained and finely minced
- coarse sea salt and freshly ground black pepper, to taste
- 1 small head cauliflower (about 450 g), green leaves trimmed and stem trimmed flush with the bottom of the head
- 1 tablespoon roughly chopped fresh flat-leaf parsley (optional)

1. In a liquid measuring jug, whisk together the olive oil, vinegar, Worcestershire, Parmesan, mustard, garlic, anchovies, and salt and pepper to taste. Place the cauliflower head upside down on a cutting board and use a paring knife to make an "x" through the full length of the core. Transfer the cauliflower head to a large bowl and pour half the dressing over it. Turn the cauliflower head to coat it in the dressing, then let it rest, stem-side up, in the dressing for at least 10 minutes and up to 30 minutes to allow the dressing to seep into all its nooks and crannies. 2. Transfer the cauliflower head, stem-side down, to the air fryer and air fry at 170°C or 25 minutes. Drizzle the remaining dressing over the cauliflower and air fry at 200°C until the top of the cauliflower is golden brown and the core is tender, about 5 minutes more. 3. Remove the basket from the air fryer and transfer the cauliflower to a large plate. Sprinkle with the parsley, if you like, and serve hot.

# Marinara Pepperoni Mushroom Pizza

**Prep time: 5 minutes | Cook time: 18 minutes | Serves 4**

- 4 large portobello mushrooms, stems removed
- 4 teaspoons olive oil
- 225 g marinara sauce
- 225 g shredded Mozzarella cheese
- 10 slices sugar-free pepperoni

1. Preheat the air fryer to 190°C. 2. Brush each mushroom cap with the olive oil, one teaspoon for each cap. 3. Put on a baking sheet and bake, stem-side down, for 8 minutes. 4. Take out of the air fryer and divide the marinara sauce, Mozzarella cheese and pepperoni evenly among the caps. 5. Air fry for another 10 minutes until browned. 6. Serve hot.

# Broccoli with Sesame Dressing

**Prep time: 5 minutes | Cook time: 10 minutes | Serves 4**

- 425 g broccoli florets, cut into bite-size pieces
- 1 tablespoon olive oil
- ¼ teaspoon salt
- 2 tablespoons sesame seeds
- 2 tablespoons rice vinegar
- 2 tablespoons coconut aminos
- 2 tablespoons sesame oil
- ½ teaspoon xylitol
- ¼ teaspoon red pepper flakes (optional)

1. Preheat the air fryer to 200°C. 2. In a large bowl, toss the broccoli with the olive oil and salt until thoroughly coated. 3. Transfer the broccoli to the air fryer basket. Pausing halfway through the cooking time to shake the basket, air fry for 10 minutes until the stems are tender and the edges are beginning to crisp. 4. Meanwhile, in the same large bowl, whisk together the sesame seeds, vinegar, coconut aminos, sesame oil, xylitol, and red pepper flakes (if using). 5. Transfer the broccoli to the bowl and toss until thoroughly coated with the seasonings. Serve warm or at room temperature.

# Sesame Carrots and Sugar Snap Peas

**Prep time: 10 minutes | Cook time: 16 minutes | Serves 4**

450 g carrots, peeled sliced on the bias (½-inch slices)
1 teaspoon olive oil
Salt and freshly ground black pepper, to taste
110 g honey
1 tablespoon sesame oil
1 tablespoon soy sauce
½ teaspoon minced fresh ginger
110 g sugar snap peas
1½ teaspoons sesame seeds

1. Preheat the air fryer to 180ºC. 2. Toss the carrots with the olive oil, season with salt and pepper and air fry for 10 minutes, shaking the basket once or twice during the cooking process. 3. Combine the honey, sesame oil, soy sauce and minced ginger in a large bowl. Add the sugar snap peas and the air-fried carrots to the honey mixture, toss to coat and return everything to the air fryer basket. 4. Turn up the temperature to 200ºC and air fry for an additional 6 minutes, shaking the basket once during the cooking process. 5. Transfer the carrots and sugar snap peas to a serving bowl. Pour the sauce from the bottom of the cooker over the vegetables and sprinkle sesame seeds over top. Serve immediately.

# Easy Rosemary Green Beans

**Prep time: 5 minutes | Cook time: 5 minutes | Serves 1**

1 tablespoon butter, melted
2 tablespoons rosemary
½ teaspoon salt
3 cloves garlic, minced
95 g chopped green beans

1. Preheat the air fryer to 200ºC. 2. Combine the melted butter with the rosemary, salt, and minced garlic. Toss in the green beans, coating them well. 3. Air fry for 5 minutes. 4. Serve immediately.

# Sweet and Crispy Roasted Pearl Onions

**Prep time: 5 minutes | Cook time: 18 minutes | Serves 3**

1 (410 g) package frozen pearl onions (do not thaw)
2 tablespoons extra-virgin olive oil
2 tablespoons balsamic vinegar
2 teaspoons finely chopped fresh rosemary
½ teaspoon coarse sea salt
¼ teaspoon black pepper

1. In a medium bowl, combine the onions, olive oil, vinegar, rosemary, salt, and pepper until well coated. 2. Transfer the onions to the air fryer basket. Set the air fryer to 200ºC for 18 minutes, or until the onions are tender and lightly charred, stirring once or twice during the cooking time.

# Chapter 6 Vegetarian Mains

# Chapter 6 Vegetarian Mains

## Cheesy Cauliflower Pizza Crust

**Prep time: 15 minutes | Cook time: 11 minutes | Serves 2**

| | |
|---|---|
| 1 (340 g) steamer bag cauliflower | 2 tablespoons blanched finely ground almond flour |
| 120 g shredded extra mature Cheddar cheese | 1 teaspoon Italian blend seasoning |
| 1 large egg | |

1. Cook cauliflower according to package instructions. 2.Remove from bag and place into cheesecloth or paper towel to remove excess water. 3.Place cauliflower into a large bowl. 4.Add cheese, egg, almond flour, and Italian seasoning to the bowl and mix well. 5.Cut a piece of parchment to fit your air fryer basket. 6.Press cauliflower into 6-inch round circle. 7.Place into the air fryer basket. 8.Adjust the temperature to 180°C and air fry for 11 minutes. 9.After 7 minutes, flip the pizza crust. 10.Add preferred toppings to pizza. 11.Place back into air fryer basket and cook an additional 4 minutes or until fully cooked and golden. 12.Serve immediately.

## Cayenne Tahini Kale

**Prep time: 5 minutes | Cook time: 15 minutes | Serves 2 to 4**

| | |
|---|---|
| Dressing: | Kale: |
| 60 ml tahini | 1 Kg packed torn kale leaves (stems and ribs removed and leaves torn into palm-size pieces) |
| 60 g fresh lemon juice | |
| 2 tablespoons olive oil | |
| 1 teaspoon sesame seeds | Rock salt and freshly ground black pepper, to taste |
| ½ teaspoon garlic powder | |
| ¼ teaspoon cayenne pepper | |

1. Preheat the air fryer to 180°C. 2.Make the dressing: Whisk together the tahini, lemon juice, olive oil, sesame seeds, garlic powder, and cayenne pepper in a large bowl until well mixed. 3.Add the kale and massage the dressing thoroughly all over the leaves. 4.Sprinkle the salt and pepper to season. 5.Place the kale in the air fryer basket in a single layer and air fry for about 15 minutes, or until the leaves are slightly wilted and crispy. 6.Remove from the basket and serve on a plate.

## Roasted Vegetables with Rice

**Prep time: 5 minutes | Cook time: 12 minutes | Serves 4**

| | |
|---|---|
| 2 teaspoons melted butter | 1 red onion, chopped |
| 235 g chopped mushrooms | 1 garlic clove, minced |
| 235 g cooked rice | Salt and black pepper, to taste |
| 235 g peas | 2 hard-boiled eggs, grated |
| 1 carrot, chopped | 1 tablespoon soy sauce |

1. Preheat the air fryer to 190°C. 2.Coat a baking dish with melted butter. 3.Stir together the mushrooms, cooked rice, peas, carrot, onion, garlic, salt, and pepper in a large bowl until well mixed. 4.Pour the mixture into the prepared baking dish and transfer to the air fryer basket. 5.Roast in the preheated air fryer for 12 minutes until the vegetables are tender. 6.Divide the mixture among four plates. 7.Serve warm with a sprinkle of grated eggs and a drizzle of soy sauce.

## Stuffed Portobellos

**Prep time: 10 minutes | Cook time: 8 minutes | Serves 4**

| | |
|---|---|
| 85 g soft white cheese | leaves |
| ½ medium courgette, trimmed and chopped | 4 large portobello mushrooms, stems removed |
| 60 g seeded and chopped red pepper | 2 tablespoons coconut oil, melted |
| 350 g chopped fresh spinach | ½ teaspoon salt |

1. In a medium bowl, mix soft white cheese, courgette, pepper, and spinach. 2.Drizzle mushrooms with coconut oil and sprinkle with salt. 3.Scoop ¼ courgette mixture into each mushroom. 4.Place mushrooms into ungreased air fryer basket. 5.Adjust the temperature to 200°C and air fry for 8 minutes. 6.Portobellos will be tender, and tops will be browned when done. 7.Serve warm.

## Baked Turnip and Courgette

**Prep time: 5 minutes | Cook time: 15 to 20 minutes | Serves 4**

| 3 turnips, sliced | 2 cloves garlic, crushed |
| 1 large courgette, sliced | 1 tablespoon olive oil |
| 1 large red onion, cut into rings | Salt and black pepper, to taste |

1. Preheat the air fryer to 170ºC. 2.Put the turnips, courgette, red onion, and garlic in a baking pan. 3.Drizzle the olive oil over the top and sprinkle with the salt and pepper. 4.Place the baking pan in the preheated air fryer and bake for 15 to 20 minutes, or until the vegetables are tender. 5.Remove from the basket and serve on a plate.

## Rice and Aubergine Bowl

**Prep time: 15 minutes | Cook time: 10 minutes | Serves 4**

| 60 g sliced cucumber | miso paste |
| 1 teaspoon salt | 1 tablespoon mirin rice wine |
| 1 tablespoon sugar | 1 Kg cooked sushi rice |
| 7 tablespoons Japanese rice vinegar | 4 spring onions |
| 3 medium aubergines, sliced | 1 tablespoon toasted sesame seeds |
| 3 tablespoons sweet white | |

1. Coat the cucumber slices with the rice wine vinegar, salt, and sugar. 2.Put a dish on top of the bowl to weight it down completely. 3.In a bowl, mix the aubergines, mirin rice wine, and miso paste. 4.Allow to marinate for half an hour. 5.Preheat the air fryer to 200ºC. 6.Put the aubergine slices in the air fryer and air fry for 10 minutes. 7.Fill the bottom of a serving bowl with rice and top with the aubergines and pickled cucumbers. 8.Add the spring onions and sesame seeds for garnish. 9.Serve immediately.

## Loaded Cauliflower Steak

**Prep time: 5 minutes | Cook time: 7 minutes | Serves 4**

| 1 medium head cauliflower | melted |
| 60 ml hot sauce | 60 g blue cheese, crumbled |
| 2 tablespoons salted butter, | 60 g full-fat ranch dressing |

1. Remove cauliflower leaves. Slice the head in ½-inch-thick slices. In a small bowl, mix hot sauce and butter. Brush the mixture over the cauliflower. 2.Place each cauliflower steak into the air fryer, working in batches if necessary. 3.Adjust the temperature to 200ºC and air fry for 7 minutes. 4.When cooked, edges will begin turning dark and caramelized. To serve, sprinkle steaks with crumbled blue cheese. 5.Drizzle with ranch dressing.

## Italian Baked Egg and Veggies

**Prep time: 10 minutes | Cook time: 10 minutes | Serves 2**

| 2 tablespoons salted butter | 1 medium plum tomato, diced |
| 1 small courgette, sliced lengthwise and quartered | 2 large eggs |
| ½ medium green pepper, seeded and diced | ¼ teaspoon onion powder |
| | ¼ teaspoon garlic powder |
| | ½ teaspoon dried basil |
| 235 g fresh spinach, chopped | ¼ teaspoon dried oregano |

1. Grease two ramekins with 1 tablespoon butter each. 2.In a large bowl, toss courgette, pepper, spinach, and tomato. 3.Divide the mixture in two and place half in each ramekin. 4.Crack an egg on top of each ramekin and sprinkle with onion powder, garlic powder, basil, and oregano. 5.Place into the air fryer basket. 6.Adjust the temperature to 170ºC and bake for 10 minutes. 7.Serve immediately.

## White Cheddar and Mushroom Soufflés

**Prep time: 15 minutes | Cook time: 12 minutes | Serves 4**

| 3 large eggs, whites and yolks separated | ¼ teaspoon salt |
| 120 g extra mature white Cheddar cheese | ¼ teaspoon ground black pepper |
| 85 g soft white cheese | 120 g chestnut mushrooms, sliced |
| ¼ teaspoon cream of tartar | |

1. In a large bowl, whip egg whites until stiff peaks form, about 2 minutes. 2.In a separate large bowl, beat Cheddar, egg yolks, soft white cheese, cream of tartar, salt, and pepper together until combined. 3.Fold egg whites into cheese mixture, being careful not to stir. 4.Fold in mushrooms, then pour mixture evenly into four ungreased ramekins. 5.Place ramekins into air fryer basket. 6.Adjust the temperature to 180ºC and bake for 12 minutes. 7.Eggs will be browned on the top and firm in the centre when done. 8.Serve warm.

# Almond-Cauliflower Gnocchi

**Prep time: 5 minutes | Cook time: 25 to 30 minutes | Serves 4**

| | |
|---|---|
| 1.2 Kg cauliflower florets | 60 g unsalted butter, melted |
| 160 g almond flour | 60 g grated Parmesan cheese |
| ½ teaspoon salt | |

1. In a food processor fitted with a metal blade, pulse the cauliflower until finely chopped. 2.Transfer the cauliflower to a large microwave-safe bowl and cover it with a paper towel. 3.Microwave for 5 minutes. 4.Spread the cauliflower on a towel to cool. 5.When cool enough to handle, draw up the sides of the towel and squeeze tightly over a sink to remove the excess moisture. 6.Return the cauliflower to the food processor and whirl until creamy. 7.Sprinkle in the flour and salt and pulse until a sticky dough comes together. 8.Transfer the dough to a workspace lightly floured with almond flour. 9.Shape the dough into a ball and divide into 4 equal sections. 10.Roll each section into a rope 1 inch thick. 11.Slice the dough into squares with a sharp knife. 12.Preheat the air fryer to 200ºC. 13.Working in batches if necessary, place the gnocchi in a single layer in the basket of the air fryer and spray generously with olive oil. 14.Pausing halfway through the cooking time to turn the gnocchi, air fry for 25 to 30 minutes until golden brown and crispy on the edges. 15.Transfer to a large bowl and toss with the melted butter and Parmesan cheese.

# Chapter 7
# Beef, Pork, and Lamb

# Chapter 7 Beef, Pork, and Lamb

## Tomato and Bacon Zoodles

**Prep time: 10 minutes | Cook time: 15 to 22 minutes | Serves 2**

| | |
|---|---|
| 230 g sliced bacon | 80 g finely grated Parmesan cheese, plus more for serving |
| 120 g baby plum tomatoes | |
| 1 large courgette, spiralized | Sea salt and freshly ground black pepper, to taste |
| 120 g ricotta cheese | |
| 60 ml double/whipping cream | |

1. Set the air fryer to 200°C. Arrange the bacon strips in a single layer in the air fryer basket—some overlapping is okay because the bacon will shrink, but cook in batches if needed. Air fry for 8 minutes. Flip the bacon strips and air fry for 2 to 5 minutes more, until the bacon is crisp. Remove the bacon from the air fryer. 2. Put the tomatoes in the air fryer basket and air fry for 3 to 5 minutes, until they are just starting to burst. Remove the tomatoes from the air fryer. 3. Put the courgette noodles in the air fryer and air fry for 2 to 4 minutes, to the desired doneness. 4. Meanwhile, combine the ricotta, cream, and Parmesan in a saucepan over medium-low heat. Cook, stirring often, until warm and combined. 5. Crumble the bacon. Place the courgette, bacon, and tomatoes in a bowl. Toss with the ricotta sauce. Season with salt and pepper, and sprinkle with additional Parmesan.

## German Rouladen-Style Steak

**Prep time: 20 minutes | Cook time: 15 minutes | Serves 4**

| | |
|---|---|
| Onion Sauce: | parsley |
| 2 medium onions, cut into ½-inch-thick slices | Rouladen: |
| | 60 ml Dijon mustard |
| Coarse or flaky salt and black pepper, to taste | 450 g bavette or skirt steak, ¼ to ½ inch thick |
| 120 ml sour cream | 1 teaspoon black pepper |
| 1 tablespoon tomato paste | 4 slices bacon |
| 2 teaspoons chopped fresh | 60 g chopped fresh parsley |

1. For the sauce: In a small bowl, mix together the onions with salt and pepper to taste. Place the onions in the air fryer basket. Set the air fryer to 200°C for 6 minutes, or until the onions are softened and golden brown. 2. Set aside half of the onions to use in the rouladen. Place the rest in a small bowl and add the sour cream, tomato paste, parsley, ½ teaspoon salt, and ½ teaspoon pepper. Stir until well combined, adding 1 to 2 tablespoons of water, if necessary, to thin the sauce slightly. Set the sauce aside. 3. For the rouladen: Evenly spread the mustard over the meat. Sprinkle with the pepper. Top with the bacon slices, reserved onions, and parsley. Starting at the long end, roll up the steak as tightly as possible, ending seam side down. Use 2 or 3 wooden toothpicks to hold the roll together. Using a sharp knife, cut the roll in half so that it better fits in the air fryer basket. 4. Place the steak, seam side down, in the air fryer basket. Set the air fryer to 200°C for 9 minutes. Use a meat thermometer to ensure the steak has reached an internal temperature of 64°C. (It is critical to not overcook bavette steak, so as to not toughen the meat.) 5. Let the steak rest for 10 minutes before cutting into slices. Serve with the sauce.

## Sausage and Pork Meatballs

**Prep time: 15 minutes | Cook time: 8 to 12 minutes | Serves 8**

| | |
|---|---|
| 1 large egg | 1 tablespoon tomato paste |
| 1 teaspoon gelatin | 1 teaspoon minced garlic |
| 450 g pork mince | 1 teaspoon dried oregano |
| 230 g Italian-seasoned sausage, casings removed, crumbled | ¼ teaspoon red pepper flakes |
| | Sea salt and freshly ground black pepper, to taste |
| 80 g Parmesan cheese | Keto-friendly marinara sauce, for serving |
| 60 g finely diced onion | |

1. Beat the egg in a small bowl and sprinkle with the gelatin. Allow to sit for 5 minutes. 2. In a large bowl, combine the pork mince, sausage, Parmesan, onion, tomato paste, garlic, oregano, and red pepper flakes. Season with salt and black pepper. 3. Stir the gelatin mixture, then add it to the other ingredients and, using clean hands, mix to ensure that everything is well combined. Form into 1½-inch round meatballs. 4. Set the air fryer to 200°C. Place the meatballs in the air fryer basket in a single layer, cooking in batches as needed. Air fry for 5 minutes. Flip and cook for 3 to 7 minutes more, or until an instant-read thermometer reads 72°C.

## Cheese Crusted Chops

**Prep time: 10 minutes | Cook time: 12 minutes | Serves 4 to 6**

| | |
|---|---|
| ¼ teaspoon pepper | ½ teaspoons onion granules |
| ½ teaspoons salt | 1 teaspoon smoked paprika |
| 4 to 6 thick boneless pork chops | 2 beaten eggs |
| 235 g pork scratching crumbs | 3 tablespoons grated Parmesan cheese |
| ¼ teaspoon chili powder | Cooking spray |

1. Preheat the air fryer to 210ºC. 2. Rub the pepper and salt on both sides of pork chops. 3. In a food processor, pulse pork scratchings into crumbs. Mix crumbs with chili powder, onion granules, and paprika in a bowl. 4. Beat eggs in another bowl. 5. Dip pork chops into eggs then into pork scratchings crumb mixture. 6. Spritz the air fryer basket with cooking spray and add pork chops to the basket. 7. Air fry for 12 minutes. 8. Serve garnished with the Parmesan cheese.

## Reuben Beef Rolls with Thousand Island Sauce

**Prep time: 15 minutes | Cook time: 10 minutes per batch | Makes 10 rolls**

| | |
|---|---|
| 230 g cooked salt beef, chopped | Thousand Island Sauce: |
| 120 g drained and chopped sauerkraut | 60 g chopped dill pickles |
| | 60 ml tomato ketchup |
| 1 (230 g) package cream cheese, softened | 180 ml mayonnaise |
| | Fresh thyme leaves, for garnish |
| 120 g shredded Swiss cheese | 2 tablespoons sugar |
| 20 slices prosciutto | ⅛ teaspoon fine sea salt |
| Cooking spray | Ground black pepper, to taste |

1. Preheat the air fryer to 200ºC and spritz with cooking spray. 2. Combine the beef, sauerkraut, cream cheese, and Swiss cheese in a large bowl. Stir to mix well. 3. Unroll a slice of prosciutto on a clean work surface, then top with another slice of prosciutto crosswise. Scoop up 4 tablespoons of the beef mixture in the center. 4. Fold the top slice sides over the filling as the ends of the roll, then roll up the long sides of the bottom prosciutto and make it into a roll shape. Overlap the sides by about 1 inch. Repeat with remaining filling and prosciutto. 5. Arrange the rolls in the preheated air fryer, seam side down, and spritz with cooking spray. 6. Air fry for 10 minutes or until golden and crispy. Flip the rolls halfway through. Work in batches to avoid overcrowding. 7. Meanwhile, combine the ingredients for the sauce in a small bowl. Stir to mix well. 8. Serve the rolls with the dipping sauce.

## Sesame Beef Lettuce Tacos

**Prep time: 30 minutes | Cook time: 8 to 10 minutes | Serves 4**

| | |
|---|---|
| 60 ml soy sauce or tamari | 450 g bavette or skirt steak |
| 60 ml avocado oil | 8 butterhead lettuce leaves |
| 2 tablespoons cooking sherry | 2 spring onions, sliced |
| 1 tablespoon granulated sweetener | 1 tablespoon toasted sesame seeds |
| 1 tablespoon ground cumin | Hot sauce, for serving |
| 1 teaspoon minced garlic | Lime wedges, for serving |
| Sea salt and freshly ground black pepper, to taste | Flaky sea salt (optional) |

1. In a small bowl, whisk together the soy sauce, avocado oil, cooking sherry, sweetener, cumin, garlic, and salt and pepper to taste. 2. Place the steak in a shallow dish. Pour the marinade over the beef. Cover the dish with plastic wrap and let it marinate in the refrigerator for at least 2 hours or overnight. 3. Remove the flank steak from the dish and discard the marinade. 4. Set the air fryer to 200ºC. Place the steak in the air fryer basket and air fry for 4 to 6 minutes. Flip the steak and cook for 4 minutes more, until an instant-read thermometer reads 49ºC at the thickest part (or cook it to your desired doneness). Allow the steak to rest for 10 minutes, then slice it thinly against the grain. 5. Stack 2 lettuce leaves on top of each other and add some sliced meat. Top with spring onions and sesame seeds. Drizzle with hot sauce and lime juice, and finish with a little flaky salt (if using). Repeat with the remaining lettuce leaves and fillings.

## Mushroom in Bacon-Wrapped Filets Mignons

**Prep time: 10 minutes | Cook time: 13 minutes per batch | Serves 8**

| | |
|---|---|
| 30 g dried porcini mushrooms | pepper |
| ½ teaspoon granulated white sugar | 8 (110 g) filets mignons or beef fillet steaks |
| ½ teaspoon salt | 8 thin-cut bacon strips |
| ½ teaspoon ground white | |

1. Preheat the air fryer to 200ºC. 2. Put the mushrooms, sugar, salt, and white pepper in a spice grinder and grind to combine. 3. On a clean work surface, rub the filets mignons with the mushroom mixture, then wrap each filet with a bacon strip. Secure with toothpicks if necessary. 4. Arrange the bacon-wrapped filets mignons in the preheated air fryer basket, seam side down. Work in batches to avoid overcrowding. 5. Air fry for 13 minutes or until medium rare. Flip the filets halfway through. 6. Serve immediately.

# Goat Cheese-Stuffed Bavette Steak

**Prep time: 10 minutes | Cook time: 14 minutes | Serves 6**

| | |
|---|---|
| 450 g bavette or skirt steak | ¼ teaspoon freshly ground black pepper |
| 1 tablespoon avocado oil | 60 g goat cheese, crumbled |
| ½ teaspoon sea salt | 235 g baby spinach, chopped |
| ½ teaspoon garlic powder | |

1. Place the steak in a large zip-top bag or between two pieces of plastic wrap. Using a meat mallet or heavy-bottomed skillet, pound the steak to an even ¼-inch thickness. 2. Brush both sides of the steak with the avocado oil. 3. Mix the salt, garlic powder, and pepper in a small dish. Sprinkle this mixture over both sides of the steak. 4. Sprinkle the goat cheese over top, and top that with the spinach. 5. Starting at one of the long sides, roll the steak up tightly. Tie the rolled steak with kitchen string at 3-inch intervals. 6. Set the air fryer to 200ºC. Place the steak roll-up in the air fryer basket. Air fry for 7 minutes. Flip the steak and cook for an additional 7 minutes, until an instant-read thermometer reads 49ºC for medium-rare (adjust the cooking time for your desired doneness).

# Chicken-Fried Steak

**Prep time: 20 minutes | Cook time: 14 minutes | Serves 2**

| | |
|---|---|
| Steak: | ½ teaspoon hot sauce |
| Oil, for spraying | 2 (140 g) minute steaks |
| 90 g all-purpose flour | Gravy: |
| 1 teaspoon salt | 2 tablespoons unsalted butter |
| 1 teaspoon freshly ground black pepper | 2 tablespoons all-purpose flour |
| ½ teaspoon paprika | 235 ml milk |
| ½ teaspoon onion granules | ½ teaspoon salt |
| 1 teaspoon granulated garlic | ½ teaspoon freshly ground black pepper |
| 180 g buttermilk | |

Make the Steak 1. Line the air fryer basket with parchment and spray lightly with oil. 2. In a medium bowl, mix together the flour, salt, black pepper, paprika, onion granules, and garlic. 3. In another bowl, whisk together the buttermilk and hot sauce. 4. Dredge the steaks in the flour mixture, dip in the buttermilk mixture, and dredge again in the flour until completely coated. Shake off any excess flour. 5. Place the steaks in the prepared basket and spray liberally with oil. 6. Air fry at 200ºC for 7 minutes, flip, spray with oil, and cook for another 6 to 7 minutes, or until crispy and browned. Make the Gravy 7. In a small saucepan, whisk together the butter and flour over medium heat until the butter is melted. Slowly add the milk, salt, and black pepper, increase the heat to medium-high, and continue to cook, stirring constantly, until the mixture thickens. Remove from the heat. 8. Transfer the steaks to plates and pour the gravy over the top. Serve immediately.

# Greek Pork with Tzatziki Sauce

**Prep time: 30 minutes | Cook time: 50 minutes | Serves 4**

| | |
|---|---|
| Greek Pork: | 2 cloves garlic, finely chopped |
| 900 g pork loin roasting joint | Tzatziki: |
| Salt and black pepper, to taste | ½ cucumber, finely chopped and squeezed |
| 1 teaspoon smoked paprika | 235 ml full-fat Greek yogurt |
| ½ teaspoon mustard seeds | 1 garlic clove, minced |
| ½ teaspoon celery salt | 1 tablespoon extra-virgin olive oil |
| 1 teaspoon fennel seeds | |
| 1 teaspoon chili powder | 1 teaspoon balsamic vinegar |
| 1 teaspoon turmeric powder | 1 teaspoon minced fresh dill |
| ½ teaspoon ground ginger | A pinch of salt |
| 2 tablespoons olive oil | |

1. Toss all ingredients for Greek pork in a large mixing bowl. Toss until the meat is well coated. 2. Cook in the preheated air fryer at 180ºC for 30 minutes; turn over and cook another 20 minutes. 3. Meanwhile, prepare the tzatziki by mixing all the tzatziki ingredients. Place in your refrigerator until ready to use. 4. Serve the pork sirloin roast with the chilled tzatziki on the side. Enjoy!

# Panko Crusted Calf's Liver Strips

**Prep time: 15 minutes | Cook time: 23 to 25 minutes | Serves 4**

| | |
|---|---|
| 450 g sliced calf's liver, cut into ½-inch wide strips | 240 g panko breadcrumbs |
| 2 eggs | Salt and ground black pepper, to taste |
| 2 tablespoons milk | Cooking spray |
| 60 g whole wheat flour | |

1. Preheat the air fryer to 200ºC and spritz with cooking spray. 2. Rub the calf's liver strips with salt and ground black pepper on a clean work surface. 3. Whisk the eggs with milk in a large bowl. Pour the flour in a shallow dish. Pour the panko on a separate shallow dish. 4. Dunk the liver strips in the flour, then in the egg mixture. Shake the excess off and roll the strips over the panko to coat well. 5. Arrange half of the liver strips in a single layer in the preheated air fryer and spritz with cooking spray. 6. Air fry for 5 minutes or until browned. Flip the strips halfway through. Repeat with the remaining strips. 7. Serve immediately.

## Italian Sausage Links

**Prep time: 10 minutes | Cook time: 24 minutes | Serves 4**

| | |
|---|---|
| 1 pepper (any color), sliced | Sea salt and freshly ground black pepper, to taste |
| 1 medium onion, sliced | |
| 1 tablespoon avocado oil | 450 g Italian-seasoned sausage links |
| 1 teaspoon Italian seasoning | |

1. Place the pepper and onion in a medium bowl, and toss with the avocado oil, Italian seasoning, and salt and pepper to taste. 2. Set the air fryer to 200°C. Put the vegetables in the air fryer basket and cook for 12 minutes. 3. Push the vegetables to the side of the basket and arrange the sausage links in the bottom of the basket in a single layer. Spoon the vegetables over the sausages. Cook for 12 minutes, tossing halfway through, until an instant-read thermometer inserted into the sausage reads 72°C.

## Bacon, Cheese and Pear Stuffed Pork

**Prep time: 10 minutes | Cook time: 24 minutes | Serves 3**

| | |
|---|---|
| 4 slices bacon, chopped | ⅛ teaspoon black pepper |
| 1 tablespoon butter | 1 pear, finely diced |
| 120 g finely diced onion | 80 g crumbled blue cheese |
| 80 g chicken stock | 3 boneless pork chops (2-inch thick) |
| 355 g seasoned stuffing mix | |
| 1 egg, beaten | Olive oil |
| ½ teaspoon dried thyme | Salt and freshly ground black pepper, to taste |
| ½ teaspoon salt | |

1. Preheat the air fryer to 200°C. 2. Place the bacon into the air fryer basket and air fry for 6 minutes, stirring halfway through the cooking time. Remove the bacon and set it aside on a paper towel. Pour out the grease from the bottom of the air fryer. 3. Make the stuffing: Melt the butter in a medium saucepan over medium heat on the stovetop. Add the onion and sauté for a few minutes, until it starts to soften. Add the chicken stock and simmer for 1 minute. Remove the pan from the heat and add the stuffing mix. Stir until the stock has been absorbed. Add the egg, dried thyme, salt and freshly ground black pepper, and stir until combined. Fold in the diced pear and crumbled blue cheese. 4. Place the pork chops on a cutting board. Using the palm of your hand to hold the chop flat and steady, slice into the side of the pork chop to make a pocket in the center of the chop. Leave about an inch of chop uncut and make sure you don't cut all the way through the pork chop. Brush both sides of the pork chops with olive oil and season with salt and freshly ground black pepper. Stuff each pork chop with a third of the stuffing, packing the stuffing tightly inside the pocket. 5. Preheat the air fryer to 180°C. 6. Spray or brush the sides of the air fryer basket with oil. Place the pork chops in the air fryer basket with the open stuffed edge of the pork chop facing the outside edges of the basket. 7. Air fry the pork chops for 18 minutes, turning the pork chops over halfway through the cooking time. When the chops are done, let them rest for 5 minutes and then transfer to a serving platter.

## Pork Loin Roast

**Prep time: 30 minutes | Cook time: 55 minutes | Serves 6**

| | |
|---|---|
| 680 g boneless pork loin joint, washed | ¾ teaspoon sea salt flakes |
| | 1 teaspoon red pepper flakes, crushed |
| 1 teaspoon mustard seeds | |
| 1 teaspoon garlic powder | 2 dried sprigs thyme, crushed |
| 1 teaspoon porcini powder | 2 tablespoons lime juice |
| 1 teaspoon onion granules | |

1. Firstly, score the meat using a small knife; make sure to not cut too deep. 2. In a small-sized mixing dish, combine all seasonings in the order listed above; mix to combine well. 3. Massage the spice mix into the pork meat to evenly distribute. Drizzle with lemon juice. 4. Set the air fryer to 180°C. Place the pork in the air fryer basket; roast for 25 to 30 minutes. Pause the machine, check for doneness and cook for 25 minutes more.

## Blackened Steak Nuggets

**Prep time: 10 minutes | Cook time: 7 minutes | Serves 2**

| | |
|---|---|
| 450 g rib eye steak, cut into 1-inch cubes | ¼ teaspoon garlic powder |
| | ¼ teaspoon onion granules |
| 2 tablespoons salted melted butter | ¼ teaspoon ground black pepper |
| ½ teaspoon paprika | ⅛ teaspoon cayenne pepper |
| ½ teaspoon salt | |

1. Place steak into a large bowl and pour in butter. Toss to coat. Sprinkle with remaining ingredients. 2. Place bites into ungreased air fryer basket. Adjust the temperature to 200°C and air fry for 7 minutes, shaking the basket three times during cooking. Steak will be crispy on the outside and browned when done and internal temperature is at least 64°C for medium and 82°C for well-done. Serve warm.

## Mozzarella Stuffed Beef and Pork Meatballs

**Prep time: 15 minutes | Cook time: 12 minutes | Serves 4 to 6**

| | |
|---|---|
| 1 tablespoon olive oil | ½ teaspoon dried oregano |
| 1 small onion, finely chopped | 1½ teaspoons salt |
| 1 to 2 cloves garlic, minced | Freshly ground black pepper, to taste |
| 340 g beef mince | 2 eggs, lightly beaten |
| 340 g pork mince | 140 g low-moisture Mozzarella or other melting cheese, cut into 1-inch cubes |
| 90 g bread crumbs | |
| 60 g grated Parmesan cheese | |
| 60 g finely chopped fresh parsley | |

1. Preheat a skillet over medium-high heat. Add the oil and cook the onion and garlic until tender, but not browned. 2. Transfer the onion and garlic to a large bowl and add the beef, pork, bread crumbs, Parmesan cheese, parsley, oregano, salt, pepper and eggs. Mix well until all the ingredients are combined. Divide the mixture into 12 evenly sized balls. Make one meatball at a time, by pressing a hole in the meatball mixture with the finger and pushing a piece of Mozzarella cheese into the hole. Mold the meat back into a ball, enclosing the cheese. 3. Preheat the air fryer to 190ºC. 4. Working in two batches, transfer six of the meatballs to the air fryer basket and air fry for 12 minutes, shaking the basket and turning the meatballs twice during the cooking process. Repeat with the remaining 6 meatballs. Serve warm.

## Italian Pork Loin

**Prep time: 30 minutes | Cook time: 16 minutes | Serves 3**

| | |
|---|---|
| 1 teaspoon sea salt | 2 garlic cloves, minced |
| ½ teaspoon black pepper, freshly cracked | 450 g pork loin joint |
| 60 ml red wine | 1 tablespoon Italian herb seasoning blend |
| 2 tablespoons mustard | |

1. In a ceramic bowl, mix the salt, black pepper, red wine, mustard, and garlic. Add the pork loin and let it marinate at least 30 minutes. 2. Spritz the sides and bottom of the air fryer basket with nonstick cooking spray. 3. Place the pork loin in the basket; sprinkle with the Italian herb seasoning blend. Cook the pork loin at 190ºC for 10 minutes. Flip halfway through, spraying with cooking oil and cook for 5 to 6 minutes more. Serve immediately.

## Lamb and Cucumber Burgers

**Prep time: 8 minutes | Cook time: 15 to 18 minutes | Serves 4**

| | |
|---|---|
| 1 teaspoon ground ginger | yogurt |
| ½ teaspoon ground coriander | 450 g lamb mince |
| ¼ teaspoon freshly ground white pepper | 1 teaspoon garlic paste |
| ½ teaspoon ground cinnamon | ¼ teaspoon salt |
| ½ teaspoon dried oregano | ¼ teaspoon freshly ground black pepper |
| ¼ teaspoon ground allspice | Cooking oil spray |
| ¼ teaspoon ground turmeric | 4 hamburger buns |
| 120 ml low-fat plain Greek | ½ cucumber, thinly sliced |

1. In a small bowl, stir together the ginger, coriander, white pepper, cinnamon, oregano, allspice, and turmeric. 2. Put the yogurt in a small bowl and add half the spice mixture. Mix well and refrigerate. 3. Insert the crisper plate into the basket and the basket into the unit. Preheat the unit by selecting AIR FRY, setting the temperature to 180ºC, and setting the time to 3 minutes. Select START/STOP to begin. 4. In a large bowl, combine the lamb, garlic paste, remaining spice mix, salt, and pepper. Gently but thoroughly mix the ingredients with your hands. Form the meat into 4 patties. 5. Once the unit is preheated, spray the crisper plate with cooking oil, and place the patties into the basket. 6. Select AIR FRY, set the temperature to 180ºC, and set the time to 18 minutes. Select START/STOP to begin. 7. After 15 minutes, check the burgers. If a food thermometer inserted into the burgers registers 72ºC, the burgers are done. If not, resume cooking. 8. When the cooking is complete, assemble the burgers on the buns with cucumber slices and a dollop of the yogurt dip.

## Parmesan Herb Filet Mignon

**Prep time: 20 minutes | Cook time: 13 minutes | Serves 4**

| | |
|---|---|
| 450 g filet mignon | 1 teaspoon dried thyme |
| Sea salt and ground black pepper, to taste | 1 tablespoon sesame oil |
| ½ teaspoon cayenne pepper | 1 small-sized egg, well-whisked |
| 1 teaspoon dried basil | 120 g Parmesan cheese, grated |
| 1 teaspoon dried rosemary | |

1. Season the filet mignon with salt, black pepper, cayenne pepper, basil, rosemary, and thyme. Brush with sesame oil. 2. Put the egg in a shallow plate. Now, place the Parmesan cheese in another plate. 3. Coat the filet mignon with the egg; then lay it into the Parmesan cheese. Set the air fryer to 180ºC. 4. Cook for 10 to 13 minutes or until golden. Serve with mixed salad leaves and enjoy!

## Parmesan-Crusted Steak

**Prep time: 30 minutes | Cook time: 12 minutes | Serves 6**

| | |
|---|---|
| 120 ml (1 stick) unsalted butter, at room temperature | almond flour |
| 235 g finely grated Parmesan cheese | 680 g sirloin steak |
| 30 g finely ground blanched | Sea salt and freshly ground black pepper, to taste |

1. Place the butter, Parmesan cheese, and almond flour in a food processor. Process until smooth. Transfer to a sheet of parchment paper and form into a log. Wrap tightly in plastic wrap. Freeze for 45 minutes or refrigerate for at least 4 hours. 2. While the butter is chilling, season the steak liberally with salt and pepper. Let the steak rest at room temperature for about 45 minutes. 3. Place the grill pan or basket in your air fryer, set it to 200ºC, and let it preheat for 5 minutes. 4. Working in batches, if necessary, place the steak on the grill pan and air fry for 4 minutes. Flip and cook for 3 minutes more, until the steak is brown on both sides. 5. Remove the steak from the air fryer and arrange an equal amount of the Parmesan butter on top of each steak. Return the steak to the air fryer and continue cooking for another 5 minutes, until an instant-read thermometer reads 49ºC for medium-rare and the crust is golden brown (or to your desired doneness). 6. Transfer the cooked steak to a plate; let rest for 10 minutes before serving.

## Bacon-Wrapped Cheese Pork

**Prep time: 10 minutes | Cook time: 20 minutes | Serves 4**

| | |
|---|---|
| 4 (1-inch-thick) boneless pork chops | cheese |
| 2 (150 g) packages Boursin | 8 slices thin-cut bacon |

1. Spray the air fryer basket with avocado oil. Preheat the air fryer to 200ºC. 2. Place one of the chops on a cutting board. With a sharp knife held parallel to the cutting board, make a 1-inch-wide incision on the top edge of the chop. Carefully cut into the chop to form a large pocket, leaving a ½-inch border along the sides and bottom. Repeat with the other 3 chops. 3. Snip the corner of a large resealable plastic bag to form a ¾-inch hole. Place the Boursin cheese in the bag and pipe the cheese into the pockets in the chops, dividing the cheese evenly among them. 4. Wrap 2 slices of bacon around each chop and secure the ends with toothpicks. Place the bacon-wrapped chops in the air fryer basket and cook for 10 minutes, then flip the chops and cook for another 8 to 10 minutes, until the bacon is crisp, the chops are cooked through, and the internal temperature reaches 64ºC. 5. Store leftovers in an airtight container in the refrigerator for up to 3 days. Reheat in a preheated 200ºC air fryer for 5 minutes, or until warmed through.

## Peppercorn-Crusted Beef Fillet

**Prep time: 10 minutes | Cook time: 25 minutes | Serves 6**

| | |
|---|---|
| 2 tablespoons salted melted butter | 3 tablespoons ground 4-peppercorn blend |
| 2 teaspoons minced roasted garlic | 1 (900 g) beef fillet, trimmed of visible fat |

1. In a small bowl, mix the butter and roasted garlic. Brush it over the beef fillet. 2. Place the ground peppercorns onto a plate and roll the fillet through them, creating a crust. Place fillet into the air fryer basket. 3. Adjust the temperature to 200ºC and roast for 25 minutes. 4. Turn the fillet halfway through the cooking time. 5. Allow meat to rest 10 minutes before slicing.

## Pork and Beef Egg Rolls

**Prep time: 30 minutes | Cook time: 7 to 8 minutes per batch | Makes 8 egg rolls**

| | |
|---|---|
| 110 g very lean beef mince | ¼ teaspoon salt |
| 110 g lean pork mince | ¼ teaspoon garlic powder |
| 1 tablespoon soy sauce | ¼ teaspoon black pepper |
| 1 teaspoon olive oil | 1 egg |
| 120 g grated carrots | 1 tablespoon water |
| 2 green onions, chopped | 8 egg roll wrappers |
| 475 g grated Chinese cabbage | Oil for misting or cooking spray |
| 60 g chopped water chestnuts | |

1. In a large skillet, brown beef and pork with soy sauce. Remove cooked meat from skillet, drain, and set aside. 2. Pour off any excess grease from skillet. Add olive oil, carrots, and onions. Sauté until barely tender, about 1 minute. 3. Stir in cabbage, cover, and cook for 1 minute or just until cabbage slightly wilts. Remove from heat. 4. In a large bowl, combine the cooked meats and vegetables, water chestnuts, salt, garlic powder, and pepper. Stir well. If needed, add more salt to taste. 5. Beat together egg and water in a small bowl. 6. Fill egg roll wrappers, using about 60 ml of filling for each wrap. Roll up and brush all over with egg wash to seal. Spray very lightly with olive oil or cooking spray. 7. Place 4 egg rolls in air fryer basket and air fry at 200ºC for 4 minutes. Turn over and cook 3 to 4 more minutes, until golden brown and crispy. 8. Repeat to cook remaining egg rolls.

# Currywurst

**Prep time: 15 minutes | Cook time: 12 minutes | Serves 4**

| | |
|---|---|
| 235 ml tomato sauce | 1 teaspoon sugar |
| 2 tablespoons cider vinegar | ¼ teaspoon cayenne pepper |
| 2 teaspoons curry powder | 1 small onion, diced |
| 2 teaspoons sweet paprika | 450 g bratwurst, sliced diagonally into 1-inch pieces |

1. In a large bowl, combine the tomato sauce, vinegar, curry powder, paprika, sugar, and cayenne. Whisk until well combined. Stir in the onion and bratwurst. 2. Transfer the mixture to a baking tray. Place the pan in the air fryer basket. Set the air fryer to 200ºC for 12 minutes, or until the sausage is heated through and the sauce is bubbling.

# Macadamia Nuts Crusted Pork Rack

**Prep time: 5 minutes | Cook time: 35 minutes | Serves 2**

| | |
|---|---|
| 1 clove garlic, minced | 1 tablespoon breadcrumbs |
| 2 tablespoons olive oil | 1 tablespoon rosemary, chopped |
| 450 g rack of pork | 1 egg |
| 235 g chopped macadamia nuts | Salt and ground black pepper, to taste |

1. Preheat the air fryer to 180ºC. 2. Combine the garlic and olive oil in a small bowl. Stir to mix well. 3. On a clean work surface, rub the pork rack with the garlic oil and sprinkle with salt and black pepper on both sides. 4. Combine the macadamia nuts, breadcrumbs, and rosemary in a shallow dish. Whisk the egg in a large bowl. 5. Dredge the pork in the egg, then roll the pork over the macadamia nut mixture to coat well. Shake the excess off. 6. Arrange the pork in the preheated air fryer and air fry for 30 minutes on both sides. Increase to 200ºC and fry for 5 more minutes or until the pork is well browned. 7. Serve immediately.

# Chapter 8
# Fish and Seafood

# Chapter 8 Fish and Seafood

## Roasted Halibut Steaks with Parsley

**Prep time: 5 minutes | Cook time: 10 minutes | Serves 4**

455 g halibut steaks
60 ml vegetable oil
2½ tablespoons Worcester sauce
2 tablespoons honey
2 tablespoons vermouth or white wine vinegar
1 tablespoon freshly squeezed lemon juice
1 tablespoon fresh parsley leaves, coarsely chopped
Salt and pepper, to taste
1 teaspoon dried basil

1. Preheat the air fryer to 200ºC. 2. Put all the ingredients in a large mixing dish and gently stir until the fish is coated evenly. 3. Transfer the fish to the air fryer basket and roast for 10 minutes, flipping the fish halfway through, or until the fish reaches an internal temperature of at least 64ºC on a meat thermometer. 4. Let the fish cool for 5 minutes and serve.

## Cucumber and Salmon Salad

**Prep time: 10 minutes | Cook time: 8 to 10 minutes | Serves 2**

455 g salmon fillet
1½ tablespoons olive oil, divided
1 tablespoon sherry vinegar
1 tablespoon capers, rinsed and drained
1 seedless cucumber, thinly sliced
¼ white onion, thinly sliced
2 tablespoons chopped fresh parsley
Salt and freshly ground black pepper, to taste

1. Preheat the air fryer to 200ºC. 2. Lightly coat the salmon with ½ tablespoon of the olive oil. Place skin-side down in the air fryer basket and air fry for 8 to 10 minutes until the fish is opaque and flakes easily with a fork. Transfer the salmon to a plate and let cool to room temperature. Remove the skin and carefully flake the fish into bite-size chunks. 3. In a small bowl, whisk the remaining 1 tablespoon olive oil and the vinegar until thoroughly combined. Add the flaked fish, capers, cucumber, onion, and parsley. Season to taste with salt and freshly ground black pepper. Toss gently to coat. Serve immediately or cover and refrigerate for up to 4 hours.

## Tuna Steak

**Prep time: 10 minutes | Cook time: 12 minutes | Serves 4**

455 g tuna steaks, boneless and cubed
1 tablespoon mustard
1 tablespoon avocado oil
1 tablespoon apple cider vinegar

1. Mix avocado oil with mustard and apple cider vinegar. 2. Then brush tuna steaks with mustard mixture and put in the air fryer basket. 3. Cook the fish at 180ºC for 6 minutes per side.

## Roasted Fish with Almond-Lemon Crumbs

**Prep time: 10 minutes | Cook time: 7 to 8 minutes | Serves 4**

70 g raw whole almonds
1 spring onion, finely chopped
Grated zest and juice of 1 lemon
½ tablespoon extra-virgin olive oil
¾ teaspoon kosher or coarse sea salt, divided
Freshly ground black pepper, to taste
4 skinless fish fillets, 170 g each
Cooking spray
1 teaspoon Dijon mustard

1. In a food processor, pulse the almonds to coarsely chop. Transfer to a small bowl and add the scallion, lemon zest, and olive oil. Season with ¼ teaspoon of the salt and pepper to taste and mix to combine. 2. Spray the top of the fish with oil and squeeze the lemon juice over the fish. Season with the remaining ½ teaspoon salt and pepper to taste. Spread the mustard on top of the fish. Dividing evenly, press the almond mixture onto the top of the fillets to adhere. 3. Preheat the air fryer to 190ºC. 4. Working in batches, place the fillets in the air fryer basket in a single layer. Air fry for 7 to 8 minutes, until the crumbs start to brown and the fish is cooked through. 5. Serve immediately.

## Coconut Prawns

**Prep time: 5 minutes | Cook time: 6 minutes | Serves 2**

| | |
|---|---|
| 230 g medium prawns, peeled and deveined | ½ teaspoon Old Bay seasoning |
| 2 tablespoons salted butter, melted | 25 g desiccated, unsweetened coconut |

1. In a large bowl, toss the prawns in butter and Old Bay seasoning. 2. Place shredded coconut in bowl. Coat each piece of prawns in the coconut and place into the air fryer basket. 3. Adjust the temperature to 200°C and air fry for 6 minutes. 4. Gently turn the prawns halfway through the cooking time. Serve immediately.

## Crunchy Air Fried Cod Fillets

**Prep time: 10 minutes | Cook time: 12 minutes | Serves 2**

| | |
|---|---|
| 20 g panko bread crumbs | parsley |
| 1 teaspoon vegetable oil | 1 tablespoon mayonnaise |
| 1 small shallot, minced | 1 large egg yolk |
| 1 small garlic clove, minced | ¼ teaspoon grated lemon zest, plus lemon wedges for serving |
| ½ teaspoon minced fresh thyme | 2 (230 g) skinless cod fillets, 1¼ inches thick |
| Salt and pepper, to taste | Vegetable oil spray |
| 1 tablespoon minced fresh | |

1. Preheat the air fryer to 150°C. 2. Make foil sling for air fryer basket by folding 1 long sheet of aluminum foil so it is 4 inches wide. Lay sheet of foil widthwise across basket, pressing foil into and up sides of basket. Fold excess foil as needed so that edges of foil are flush with top of basket. Lightly spray the foil and basket with vegetable oil spray. 3. Toss the panko with the oil in a bowl until evenly coated. Stir in the shallot, garlic, thyme, ¼ teaspoon salt, and ⅛ teaspoon pepper. Microwave, stirring frequently, until the panko is light golden brown, about 2 minutes. Transfer to a shallow dish and let cool slightly; stir in the parsley. Whisk the mayonnaise, egg yolk, lemon zest, and ⅛ teaspoon pepper together in another bowl. 4. Pat the cod dry with paper towels and season with salt and pepper. Arrange the fillets, skinned-side down, on plate and brush tops evenly with mayonnaise mixture. (Tuck thinner tail ends of fillets under themselves as needed to create uniform pieces.) Working with 1 fillet at a time, dredge the coated side in panko mixture, pressing gently to adhere. Arrange the fillets, crumb-side up, on sling in the prepared basket, spaced evenly apart. 5. Bake for 12 to 16 minutes, using a sling to rotate fillets halfway through cooking. Using a sling, carefully remove cod from air fryer. Serve with the lemon wedges.

## Trout Amandine with Lemon Butter Sauce

**Prep time: 20 minutes | Cook time: 8 minutes | Serves 4**

| | |
|---|---|
| Trout Amandine: | Lemon Butter Sauce: |
| 65 g toasted almonds | 8 tablespoons butter, melted |
| 30 g grated Parmesan cheese | 2 tablespoons freshly squeezed lemon juice |
| 1 teaspoon salt | ½ teaspoon Worcestershire sauce |
| ½ teaspoon freshly ground black pepper | ½ teaspoon salt |
| 2 tablespoons butter, melted | ½ teaspoon freshly ground black pepper |
| 4 trout fillets, or salmon fillets, 110 g each | ¼ teaspoon hot sauce |
| Cooking spray | |

1. In a blender or food processor, pulse the almonds for 5 to 10 seconds until finely processed. Transfer to a shallow bowl and whisk in the Parmesan cheese, salt, and pepper. Place the melted butter in another shallow bowl. 2. One at a time, dip the fish in the melted butter, then the almond mixture, coating thoroughly. 3. Preheat the air fryer to 150°C. Line the air fryer basket with baking paper. 4. Place the coated fish on the baking paper and spritz with oil. 5. Bake for 4 minutes. Flip the fish, spritz it with oil, and bake for 4 minutes more until the fish flakes easily with a fork. 6. In a small bowl, whisk the butter, lemon juice, Worcestershire sauce, salt, pepper, and hot sauce until blended. 7. Serve with the fish.

## Golden Prawns

**Prep time: 20 minutes | Cook time: 7 minutes | Serves 4**

| | |
|---|---|
| 2 egg whites | 1 teaspoon garlic powder |
| 30 g coconut flour | ½ teaspoon dried rosemary |
| 120 g Parmigiano-Reggiano, grated | ½ teaspoon sea salt |
| ½ teaspoon celery seeds | ½ teaspoon ground black pepper |
| ½ teaspoon porcini powder | 680 g prawns, peeled and deveined |
| ½ teaspoon onion powder | |

1. Whisk the egg with coconut flour and Parmigiano-Reggiano. Add in seasonings and mix to combine well. 2. Dip your prawns in the batter. Roll until they are covered on all sides. 3. Cook in the preheated air fryer at 200°C for 5 to 7 minutes or until golden brown. Work in batches. Serve with lemon wedges if desired.

## Easy Scallops

**Prep time: 5 minutes | Cook time: 4 minutes | Serves 2**

| | |
|---|---|
| 12 medium sea scallops, rinsed and patted dry | pepper, plus more for garnish |
| 1 teaspoon fine sea salt | Fresh thyme leaves, for garnish (optional) |
| ¾ teaspoon ground black | Avocado oil spray |

1. Preheat the air fryer to 200ºC. Coat the air fryer basket with avocado oil spray. 2. Place the scallops in a medium bowl and spritz with avocado oil spray. Sprinkle the salt and pepper to season. 3. Transfer the seasoned scallops to the air fryer basket, spacing them apart. You may need to work in batches to avoid overcrowding. 4. Air fry for 4 minutes, flipping the scallops halfway through, or until the scallops are firm and reach an internal temperature of just 64ºC on a meat thermometer. 5. Remove from the basket and repeat with the remaining scallops. 6. Sprinkle the pepper and thyme leaves on top for garnish, if desired. Serve immediately.

## Parmesan Mackerel with Coriander

**Prep time: 10 minutes | Cook time: 7 minutes | Serves 2**

| | |
|---|---|
| 340 g mackerel fillet | 1 teaspoon ground coriander |
| 60 g Parmesan, grated | 1 tablespoon olive oil |

1. Sprinkle the mackerel fillet with olive oil and put it in the air fryer basket. 2. Top the fish with ground coriander and Parmesan. 3. Cook the fish at 200ºC for 7 minutes.

## Confetti Salmon Burgers

**Prep time: 10 minutes | Cook time: 12 minutes | Serves 4**

| | |
|---|---|
| 400 g cooked fresh or canned salmon, flaked with a fork | 1 teaspoon crab boil seasoning such as Old Bay |
| 40 g minced spring onions, white and light green parts only | ½ teaspoon kosher or coarse sea salt |
| 40 g minced red bell pepper | ½ teaspoon black pepper |
| 40 g minced celery | 1 egg, beaten |
| 2 small lemons | 20 g fresh bread crumbs |
| | Vegetable oil, for spraying |

1. In a large bowl, combine the salmon, vegetables, the zest and juice of 1 of the lemons, crab boil seasoning, salt, and pepper. Add the egg and bread crumbs and stir to combine. Form the mixture into 4 patties weighing approximately 140 g each. Chill until firm, about 15 minutes. 2. Preheat the air fryer to 200ºC. 3. Spray the salmon patties with oil on all sides and spray the air fryer basket to prevent sticking. Air fry for 12 minutes, flipping halfway through, until the burgers are browned and cooked through. Cut the remaining lemon into 4 wedges and serve with the burgers.

## Tex-Mex Salmon Bowl

**Prep time: 15 minutes | Cook time: 9 to 14 minutes | Serves 4**

| | |
|---|---|
| 340 g salmon fillets, cut into 1½-inch cubes | 60 ml salsa |
| 1 red onion, chopped | 2 teaspoons peanut or safflower oil |
| 1 jalapeño pepper, minced | 2 tablespoons tomato juice |
| 1 red bell pepper, chopped | 1 teaspoon chilli powder |

1. Preheat the air fryer to 190ºC. 2. Mix together the salmon cubes, red onion, jalapeño, red bell pepper, salsa, peanut oil, tomato juice, chilli powder in a medium metal bowl and stir until well incorporated. 3. Transfer the bowl to the air fryer basket and bake for 9 to 14 minutes, stirring once, or until the salmon is cooked through and the veggies are fork-tender. 4. Serve warm.

## Baked Monkfish

**Prep time: 20 minutes | Cook time: 12 minutes | Serves 2**

| | |
|---|---|
| 2 teaspoons olive oil | or tamari |
| 100 g celery, sliced | 2 tablespoons lime juice |
| 2 bell peppers, sliced | Coarse salt and ground black pepper, to taste |
| 1 teaspoon dried thyme | 1 teaspoon cayenne pepper |
| ½ teaspoon dried marjoram | 90 g Kalamata olives, pitted and sliced |
| ½ teaspoon dried rosemary | |
| 2 monkfish fillets | |
| 1 tablespoon coconut aminos, | |

1. In a nonstick skillet, heat the olive oil for 1 minute. Once hot, sauté the celery and peppers until tender, about 4 minutes. Sprinkle with thyme, marjoram, and rosemary and set aside. 2. Toss the fish fillets with the coconut aminos, lime juice, salt, black pepper, and cayenne pepper. Place the fish fillets in the lightly greased air fryer basket and bake at 200ºC for 8 minutes. 3. Turn them over, add the olives, and cook an additional 4 minutes. Serve with the sautéed vegetables on the side. Bon appétit!

# Baked Salmon with Tomatoes and Olives

**Prep time: 5 minutes | Cook time: 8 minutes | Serves 4**

| | |
|---|---|
| 2 tablespoons olive oil | 1 teaspoon chopped fresh dill |
| 4 (1½-inch-thick) salmon fillets | 2 plum tomatoes, diced |
| ½ teaspoon salt | 45 g sliced Kalamata olives |
| ¼ teaspoon cayenne | 4 lemon slices |

1. Preheat the air fryer to 190°C. 2. Brush the olive oil on both sides of the salmon fillets, and then season them lightly with salt, cayenne, and dill. 3. Place the fillets in a single layer in the basket of the air fryer, then layer the tomatoes and olives over the top. Top each fillet with a lemon slice. 4. Bake for 8 minutes, or until the salmon has reached an internal temperature of 64°C.

# Almond Catfish

**Prep time: 10 minutes | Cook time: 12 minutes | Serves 4**

| | |
|---|---|
| 900 g catfish fillet | 1 teaspoon salt |
| 25 g almond flour | 1 teaspoon avocado oil |
| 2 eggs, beaten | |

1. Sprinkle the catfish fillet with salt and dip in the eggs. 2. Then coat the fish in the almond flour and put in the air fryer basket. Sprinkle the fish with avocado oil. 3. Cook the fish for 6 minutes per side at 190°C.

# Stuffed Sole Florentine

**Prep time: 10 minutes | Cook time: 25 minutes | Serves 4**

| | |
|---|---|
| 40 g pine nuts | pepper, to taste |
| 2 tablespoons olive oil | 2 tablespoons unsalted butter, divided |
| 90 g chopped tomatoes | |
| 170 g bag spinach, coarsely chopped | 4 Sole fillets (about 680 g) |
| 2 cloves garlic, chopped | Dash of paprika |
| Salt and freshly ground black | ½ lemon, sliced into 4 wedges |

1. Place the pine nuts in a baking dish that fits in your air fryer. Set the air fryer to 200°C and air fry for 4 minutes until the nuts are lightly browned and fragrant. Remove the baking dish from the air fryer, tip the nuts onto a plate to cool, and continue preheating the air fryer. When the nuts are cool enough to handle, chop them into fine pieces. 2. In the baking dish, combine the oil, tomatoes, spinach, and garlic. Use tongs to toss until thoroughly combined. Air fry for 5 minutes until the tomatoes are softened and the spinach is wilted. 3. Transfer the vegetables to a bowl and stir in the toasted pine nuts. Season to taste with salt and freshly ground black pepper. 4. Place 1 tablespoon of the butter in the bottom of the baking dish. Lower the heat on the air fryer to 180°C. 5. Place the sole on a clean work surface. Sprinkle both sides with salt and black pepper. Divide the vegetable mixture among the sole fillets and carefully roll up, securing with toothpicks. 6. Working in batches if necessary, arrange the fillets seam-side down in the baking dish along with 1 tablespoon of water. Top the fillets with remaining 1 tablespoon butter and sprinkle with a dash of paprika. 7. Cover loosely with foil and air fry for 10 to 15 minutes until the fish is opaque and flakes easily with a fork. Remove the toothpicks before serving with the lemon wedges.

# Sesame-Crusted Tuna Steak

**Prep time: 5 minutes | Cook time: 8 minutes | Serves 2**

| | |
|---|---|
| 2 tuna steaks, 170 g each | 2 teaspoons white sesame seeds |
| 1 tablespoon coconut oil, melted | 2 teaspoons black sesame seeds |
| ½ teaspoon garlic powder | |

1. Brush each tuna steak with coconut oil and sprinkle with garlic powder. 2. In a large bowl, mix sesame seeds and then press each tuna steak into them, covering the steak as completely as possible. Place tuna steaks into the air fryer basket. 3. Adjust the temperature to 200°C and air fry for 8 minutes. 4. Flip the steaks halfway through the cooking time. Steaks will be well-done at 64°C internal temperature. Serve warm.

# Prawn Bake

**Prep time: 15 minutes | Cook time: 5 minutes | Serves 4**

| | |
|---|---|
| 400 g prawns, peeled and deveined | 120 g Cheddar cheese, shredded |
| 1 egg, beaten | ½ teaspoon coconut oil |
| 120 ml coconut milk | 1 teaspoon ground coriander |

1. In the mixing bowl, mix prawns with egg, coconut milk, Cheddar cheese, coconut oil, and ground coriander. 2. Then put the mixture in the baking ramekins and put in the air fryer. 3. Cook the prawns at 200°C for 5 minutes.

## Garlic Butter Prawns Scampi

**Prep time: 5 minutes | Cook time: 8 minutes | Serves 4**

| Sauce: | 1 tablespoon chopped fresh |
| 60 g unsalted butter | parsley, plus more for garnish |
| 2 tablespoons fish stock or | 1 teaspoon red pepper flakes |
| chicken broth | Prawns: |
| 2 cloves garlic, minced | 455 g large prawns, peeled |
| 2 tablespoons chopped fresh | and deveined, tails removed |
| basil leaves | Fresh basil sprigs, for garnish |
| 1 tablespoon lemon juice | |

1. Preheat the air fryer to 180°C. 2. Put all the ingredients for the sauce in a baking pan and stir to incorporate. 3. Transfer the baking pan to the air fryer and air fry for 3 minutes, or until the sauce is heated through. 4. Once done, add the prawns to the baking pan, flipping to coat in the sauce. 5. Return to the air fryer and cook for another 5 minutes, or until the prawns are pink and opaque. Stir the prawns twice during cooking. 6. Serve garnished with the parsley and basil sprigs.

## Fish Tacos with Jalapeño-Lime Sauce

**Prep time: 25 minutes | Cook time: 7 to 10 minutes | Serves 4**

| Fish Tacos: | 120 ml sour cream |
| 455 g firm white fish fillets | 1 tablespoon lime juice |
| ¼ teaspoon cumin | ¼ teaspoon grated lime zest |
| ¼ teaspoon coriander | ½ teaspoon minced jalapeño |
| ⅛ teaspoon ground red pepper | (flesh only) |
| 1 tablespoon lime zest | ¼ teaspoon cumin |
| ¼ teaspoon smoked paprika | Napa Cabbage Garnish: |
| 1 teaspoon oil | 90 g shredded Savoy cabbage |
| Cooking spray | 40 g sliced red or green bell |
| 6 to 8 corn or flour tortillas (6-inch size) | pepper |
| Jalapeño-Lime Sauce: | 30 g sliced onion |

1. Slice the fish fillets into strips approximately ½-inch thick. 2. Put the strips into a sealable plastic bag along with the cumin, coriander, red pepper, lime zest, smoked paprika, and oil. Massage seasonings into the fish until evenly distributed. 3. Spray the air fryer basket with nonstick cooking spray and place seasoned fish inside. 4. Air fry at 200°C for approximately 5 minutes. Shake basket to distribute fish. Cook an additional 2 to 5 minutes, until fish flakes easily. 5. While the fish is cooking, prepare the Jalapeño-Lime Sauce by mixing the sour cream, lime juice, lime zest, jalapeño, and cumin together to make a smooth sauce. Set aside. 6. Mix the cabbage, bell pepper, and onion together and set aside. 7. To warm refrigerated tortillas, wrap in damp paper towels and microwave for 30 to 60 seconds. 8. To serve, spoon some of fish into a warm tortilla. Add one or two tablespoons Napa Cabbage Garnish and drizzle with Jalapeño-Lime Sauce.

## Country Prawns

**Prep time: 10 minutes | Cook time: 15 to 20 minutes | Serves 4**

| 455 g large prawns, peeled | 1 red bell pepper, cut into |
| and deveined, with tails on | chunks |
| 455 g smoked sausage, cut | 1 tablespoon Old Bay |
| into thick slices | seasoning |
| 2 corn cobs, quartered | 2 tablespoons olive oil |
| 1 courgette, cut into bite-sized | Cooking spray |
| pieces | |

1. Preheat the air fryer to 200°C. Spray the air fryer basket lightly with cooking spray. 2. In a large bowl, mix the prawns, sausage, corn, courgette, bell pepper, and Old Bay seasoning, and toss to coat with the spices. Add the olive oil and toss again until evenly coated. 3. Spread the mixture in the air fryer basket in a single layer. You will need to cook in batches. 4. Air fry for 15 to 20 minutes, or until cooked through, shaking the basket every 5 minutes for even cooking. 5. Serve immediately.

## Almond-Crusted Fish

**Prep time: 15 minutes | Cook time: 10 minutes | Serves 4**

| 4 firm white fish fillets, 110g | Salt and pepper, to taste |
| each | 470 g plain flour |
| 25 g breadcrumbs | 1 egg, beaten with 1 |
| 20 g slivered almonds, | tablespoon water |
| crushed | Olive or vegetable oil for |
| 2 tablespoons lemon juice | misting or cooking spray |
| ⅛ teaspoon cayenne | |

1. Split fish fillets lengthwise down the center to create 8 pieces. 2. Mix breadcrumbs and almonds together and set aside. 3. Mix the lemon juice and cayenne together. Brush on all sides of fish. 4. Season fish to taste with salt and pepper. 5. Place the flour on a sheet of wax paper. 6. Roll fillets in flour, dip in egg wash, and roll in the crumb mixture. 7. Mist both sides of fish with oil or cooking spray. 8. Spray the air fryer basket and lay fillets inside. 9. Roast at 200°C for 5 minutes, turn fish over, and cook for an additional 5 minutes or until fish is done and flakes easily.

## Tuna-Stuffed Tomatoes

**Prep time: 5 minutes | Cook time: 5 minutes | Serves 2**

| | |
|---|---|
| 2 medium beefsteak tomatoes, tops removed, seeded, membranes removed | 2 tablespoons mayonnaise |
| | ¼ teaspoon salt |
| | ¼ teaspoon ground black pepper |
| 2 (75 g) g tuna fillets packed in water, drained | 2 teaspoons coconut oil |
| 1 medium stalk celery, trimmed and chopped | 25 g shredded mild Cheddar cheese |

1. Scoop pulp out of each tomato, leaving ½-inch shell. 2. In a medium bowl, mix tuna, celery, mayonnaise, salt, and pepper. Drizzle with coconut oil. Spoon ½ mixture into each tomato and top each with 2 tablespoons Cheddar. 3. Place tomatoes into ungreased air fryer basket. Adjust the temperature to 160°C and air fry for 5 minutes. Cheese will be melted when done. Serve warm.

## Sea Bass with Potato Scales

**Prep time: 10 minutes | Cook time: 10 minutes | Serves 2**

| | |
|---|---|
| 2 fillets of sea bass, 170- to 230 g each | very thinly sliced into rounds |
| | Olive oil |
| Salt and freshly ground black pepper, to taste | ½ clove garlic, crushed into a paste |
| 60 ml mayonnaise | 1 tablespoon capers, drained and rinsed |
| 2 teaspoons finely chopped lemon zest | 1 tablespoon olive oil |
| 1 teaspoon chopped fresh thyme | 1 teaspoon lemon juice, to taste |
| 2 Fingerling, or new potatoes, | |

1. Preheat the air fryer to 200°C. 2. Season the fish well with salt and freshly ground black pepper. Mix the mayonnaise, lemon zest and thyme together in a small bowl. Spread a thin layer of the mayonnaise mixture on both fillets. Start layering rows of potato slices onto the fish fillets to simulate the fish scales. The second row should overlap the first row slightly. Dabbing a little more mayonnaise along the upper edge of the row of potatoes where the next row overlaps will help the potato slices stick. Press the potatoes onto the fish to secure them well and season again with salt. Brush or spray the potato layer with olive oil. 3. Transfer the fish to the air fryer and air fry for 8 to 10 minutes, depending on the thickness of your fillets. 1-inch of fish should take 10 minutes at 200°C. 4. While the fish is cooking, add the garlic, capers, olive oil and lemon juice to the remaining mayonnaise mixture to make the caper aïoli. 5. Serve the fish warm with a dollop of the aïoli on top or on the side.

## Sole and Cauliflower Fritters

**Prep time: 5 minutes | Cook time: 24 minutes | Serves 2**

| | |
|---|---|
| 230 g sole fillets | 1 tablespoon olive oil |
| 230 g mashed cauliflower | 1 tablespoon coconut aminos or tamari |
| 75 g red onion, chopped | |
| 1 bell pepper, finely chopped | ½ teaspoon scotch bonnet pepper, minced |
| 1 egg, beaten | |
| 2 garlic cloves, minced | ½ teaspoon paprika |
| 2 tablespoons fresh parsley, chopped | Salt and white pepper, to taste |
| | Cooking spray |

1. Preheat the air fryer to 200°C. Spray the air fryer basket with cooking spray. 2. Place the sole fillets in the basket and air fry for 10 minutes, flipping them halfway through. 3. When the fillets are done, transfer them to a large bowl. Mash the fillets into flakes. Add the remaining ingredients and stir to combine. 4. Make the fritters: Scoop out 2 tablespoons of the fish mixture and shape into a patty about ½ inch thick with your hands. Repeat with the remaining fish mixture. 5. Arrange the patties in the air fryer basket and bake for 14 minutes, flipping the patties halfway through, or until they are golden brown and cooked through. 6. Cool for 5 minutes and serve on a plate.

# Chapter 9
# Snacks and Appetizers

# Chapter 9 Snacks and Appetizers

## Crispy Green Bean Fries with Lemon-Yoghurt Sauce

**Prep time: 5 minutes | Cook time: 5 minutes | Serves 4**

| French beans: | 227 g whole French beans |
|---|---|
| 1 egg | Lemon-Yoghurt Sauce: |
| 2 tablespoons water | 120 ml non-fat plain Greek yoghurt |
| 1 tablespoon wholemeal flour | 1 tablespoon lemon juice |
| ¼ teaspoon paprika | ¼ teaspoon salt |
| ½ teaspoon garlic powder | ⅛ teaspoon cayenne pepper |
| ½ teaspoon salt | |
| 25 g wholemeal breadcrumbs | |

Make the French beans: 1. Preheat the air fryer to 190°C. 2. In a medium shallow dish, beat together the egg and water until frothy. 3. In a separate medium shallow dish, whisk together the flour, paprika, garlic powder, and salt, then mix in the breadcrumbs. 4. Spray the bottom of the air fryer with cooking spray. 5. Dip each green bean into the egg mixture, then into the bread crumb mixture, coating the outside with the crumbs. Place the French beans in a single layer in the bottom of the air fryer basket. 6. Fry in the air fryer for 5 minutes, or until the breading is golden. Make the Lemon-Yoghurt Sauce: 7. In a small bowl, combine the yoghurt, lemon juice, salt, and cayenne. 8. Serve the green bean fries alongside the lemon-yoghurt sauce as a snack or appetizer.

## Greens Chips with Curried Yoghurt Sauce

**Prep time: 10 minutes | Cook time: 5 to 6 minutes | Serves 4**

| 240 ml low-fat Greek yoghurt | leaves cut into 2- to 3-inch pieces |
|---|---|
| 1 tablespoon freshly squeezed lemon juice | ½ bunch chard, stemmed, ribs removed and discarded, leaves cut into 2- to 3-inch pieces |
| 1 tablespoon curry powder | |
| ½ bunch curly kale, stemmed, ribs removed and discarded, | 1½ teaspoons olive oil |

1. In a small bowl, stir together the yoghurt, lemon juice, and curry powder. Set aside. 2. In a large bowl, toss the kale and chard with the olive oil, working the oil into the leaves with your hands. This helps break up the fibres in the leaves so the chips are tender. 3. Air fry the greens in batches at 200°C for 5 to 6 minutes, until crisp, shaking the basket once during cooking. Serve with the yoghurt sauce.

## Easy Spiced Nuts

**Prep time: 5 minutes | Cook time: 25 minutes | Makes 3 L**

| 1 egg white, lightly beaten | ¼ teaspoon ground allspice |
|---|---|
| 48 g sugar | Pinch ground cayenne pepper |
| 1 teaspoon salt | 100 g pecan halves |
| ½ teaspoon cinnamon powder | 135 g cashews |
| ¼ teaspoon ground cloves | 140 g almonds |

1. Combine the egg white with the sugar and spices in a bowl. 2. Preheat the air fryer to 150°C. 3. Spray or brush the air fryer basket with mixed vegetables oil. Toss the nuts together in the spiced egg white and transfer the nuts to the air fryer basket. 4. Air fry for 25 minutes, stirring the nuts in the basket a few times during the cooking process. Taste the nuts (carefully because they will be very hot) to see if they are crunchy and nicely toasted. Air fry for a few more minutes if necessary. 5. Serve warm or cool to at room temperature and store in an airtight container for up to two weeks.

## Spicy Chicken Bites

**Prep time: 10 minutes | Cook time: 10 to 12 minutes | Makes 30 bites**

| 227 g boneless and skinless chicken thighs, cut into 30 pieces | ¼ teaspoon rock salt |
|---|---|
| | 2 tablespoons hot sauce |
| | Cooking spray |

1. Preheat the air fryer to 200°C. 2. Spray the air fryer basket with cooking spray and season the chicken bites with the rock salt, then place in the basket and air fry for 10 to 12 minutes or until crispy. 3. While the chicken bites cook, pour the hot sauce into a large bowl. 4. Remove the bites and add to the sauce bowl, tossing to coat. Serve warm.

## Baked Spanakopita Dip

**Prep time: 10 minutes | Cook time: 15 minutes | Serves 2**

| | |
|---|---|
| Olive oil cooking spray | divided |
| 3 tablespoons olive oil, divided | Zest of 1 lemon |
| 2 tablespoons minced white onion | ¼ teaspoon ground nutmeg |
| 2 garlic cloves, minced | 1 teaspoon dried fresh dill weed |
| 100 g fresh spinach | ½ teaspoon salt |
| 113 g soft white cheese, softened | Pitta chips, carrot sticks, or sliced bread for serving (optional) |
| 113 g feta cheese cheese, | |

1. Preheat the air fryer to 180ºC. Coat the inside of a 6-inch ramekin or baking dish with olive oil cooking spray. 2. In a large frying pan over medium heat, heat 1 tablespoon of the olive oil. Add the onion, then cook for 1 minute. 3. Add in the garlic and cook, stirring for 1 minute more. 4. Reduce the heat to low and mix in the spinach and water. Let this cook for 2 to 3 minutes, or until the spinach has wilted. Remove the frying pan from the heat. 5. In a medium-sized bowl, combine the soft white cheese, 57 g of the feta cheese, and the remaining 2 tablespoons of olive oil, along with the lemon zest, nutmeg, fresh dill, and salt. Mix until just combined. 6. Add the mixed vegetables to the cheese base and stir until combined. 7. Pour the dip mixture into the prepared ramekin and top with the remaining 57 g of feta cheese cheese. 8. Place the dip into the air fryer basket and cook for 10 minutes, or until heated through and bubbling. 9. Serve with pitta chips, carrot sticks, or sliced bread.

## Lebanese Muhammara

**Prep time: 15 minutes | Cook time: 15 minutes | Serves 6**

| | |
|---|---|
| 2 large red peppers | 1 teaspoon rock salt |
| 60 ml plus 2 tablespoons extra-virgin olive oil | 1 teaspoon red pepper flakes |
| 85 g walnut halves | Raw mixed vegetables (such as cucumber, carrots, sliced courgette, or cauliflower) or toasted pitta bread chips, for serving |
| 1 tablespoon agave syrup or honey | |
| 1 teaspoon fresh lemon juice | |
| 1 teaspoon cumin powder | |

1. Drizzle the peppers with 2 tablespoons of the olive oil and place in the air fryer basket. Set the air fryer to 200ºC for 10 minutes. 2. Add the walnuts to the basket, arranging them around the peppers. Set the air fryer to 200ºC for 5 minutes. 3. Remove the peppers, seal in a a resealable plastic bag, and let rest for 5 to 10 minutes. Transfer the walnuts to a plate and set aside to cool down. 4. Place the softened peppers, walnuts, agave, lemon juice, cumin, salt, and ½ teaspoon of the pepper flakes blend in a food processor until smooth. 5. Transfer the dip to a serving bowl and create an indentation in the middle. Pour the remaining 60 ml olive oil into the indentation. Garnish the dip with the remaining ½ teaspoon pepper flakes. 6. Serve with mixed vegetables or toasted pitta bread chips.

## Veggie Salmon Nachos

**Prep time: 10 minutes | Cook time: 9 to 12 minutes | Serves 6**

| | |
|---|---|
| 57 g baked no-salt sweetcorn tortilla chips | 50 g grated carrot |
| 1 (142 g) baked salmon fillet, flaked | 1 jalapeño chillies pepper, minced |
| 100 g canned low-salt black beans, rinsed and drained | 30 g shredded low-salt low-fat Swiss cheese |
| 1 red pepper, chopped | 1 tomato, chopped |

1. Preheat the air fryer to 180ºC. 2. In a baking pan, layer the tortilla chips. Top with the salmon, black beans, red pepper, carrot, jalapeño chillies, and Swiss cheese. 3. Bake in the air fryer for 9 to 12 minutes, or until the cheese is melted and starts to brown. 4. Top with the tomato and serve.

## Crispy Cajun Fresh Dill Pickle Chips

**Prep time: 5 minutes | Cook time: 10 minutes | Makes 16 slices**

| | |
|---|---|
| 30 g plain flour | 2 large fresh dill pickled cucumbers, sliced into 8 rounds each |
| 42 g panko breadcrumbs | |
| 1 large egg, beaten | |
| 2 teaspoons Cajun seasoning | Cooking spray |

1. Preheat the air fryer to 200ºC. 2. Place the plain flour, panko breadcrumbs, and egg into 3 separate shallow dishes, then stir the Cajun seasoning into the flour. 3. Dredge each pickle chip in the flour mixture, then the egg, and finally the breadcrumbs. Shake off any excess, then place each coated pickle chip on a plate. 4. Spritz the air fryer basket with cooking spray, then place 8 pickle chips in the basket and air fry for 5 minutes, or until crispy and golden. Repeat this process with the remaining pickle chips. 5. Remove the chips and allow to slightly cool on a a wire rack before serving.

# Italian Rice Balls

**Prep time: 20 minutes | Cook time: 10 minutes | Makes 8 rice balls**

| | |
|---|---|
| 355 g cooked sticky rice | (small enough to stuff into olives) |
| ½ teaspoon Italian seasoning blend | 2 eggs |
| ¾ teaspoon salt, divided | 35 g Italian breadcrumbs |
| 8 black olives, pitted | 55 g panko breadcrumbs |
| 28 g mozzarella cheese cheese, cut into tiny pieces | Cooking spray |

1. Preheat air fryer to 200ºC. 2. Stuff each black olive with a piece of mozzarella cheese cheese. Set aside. 3. In a bowl, combine the cooked sticky rice, Italian seasoning blend, and ½ teaspoon of salt and stir to mix well. Form the rice mixture into a log with your hands and divide it into 8 equal portions. Mould each portion around a black olive and roll into a ball. 4. Transfer to the freezer to chill for 10 to 15 minutes until firm. 5. In a shallow dish, place the Italian breadcrumbs. In a separate shallow dish, whisk the eggs. In a third shallow dish, combine the panko breadcrumbs and remaining salt. 6. One by one, roll the rice balls in the Italian breadcrumbs, then dip in the whisked eggs, finally coat them with the panko breadcrumbs. 7. Arrange the rice balls in the air fryer basket and spritz both sides with cooking spray. 8. Air fry for 10 minutes until the rice balls are golden. Flip the balls halfway through the cooking time. 9. Serve warm.

# Parmesan Chips

**Prep time: 10 minutes | Cook time: 15 minutes per batch | Serves 2**

| | |
|---|---|
| 2 to 3 large russet potatoes or Maris Piper potatoes, peeled and cut into ½-inch sticks | ½ teaspoon salt |
| | Freshly ground black pepper, to taste |
| 2 teaspoons mixed vegetables or rapeseed oil | 1 teaspoon fresh chopped parsley |
| 50 g grated Parmesan cheese | |

1. Bring a large saucepan of salted water to a boil on the hop while you peel and cut the potatoes. Blanch the potatoes in the boiling salted water for 4 minutes while you preheat the air fryer to 200ºC. Strain the potatoes and rinse them with cold water. Dry them well with a clean kitchen towel. 2. Toss the dried potato sticks gently with the oil and place them in the air fryer basket. Air fry for 25 minutes, shaking the basket a few times while the fries cook to help them brown evenly. 3. Combine the Parmesan cheese, salt and pepper. With 2 minutes left on the air fryer cooking time, sprinkle the fries with the Parmesan cheese mixture. Toss the fries to coat them evenly with the cheese mixture and continue to air fry for the final 2 minutes, until the cheese has melted and just starts to brown. Sprinkle the finished fries with chopped parsley, a little more grated Parmesan cheese if you like, and serve.

# Pepperoni Pizza Dip

**Prep time: 10 minutes | Cook time: 10 minutes | Serves 6**

| | |
|---|---|
| 170 g soft white cheese | 42 g sliced miniature pepperoni |
| 85 g shredded Italian cheese blend | 400 g sliced black olives |
| 60 ml soured cream | 1 tablespoon thinly sliced spring onion |
| 1½ teaspoons dried Italian seasoning | Cut-up raw mixed vegetables, toasted baguette slices, pitta chips, or tortilla chips, for serving |
| ¼ teaspoon garlic salt | |
| ¼ teaspoon onion powder | |
| 165 g pizza sauce | |

1. In a small bowl, combine the soft white cheese, 28 g of the shredded cheese, the soured cream, Italian seasoning, garlic salt, and onion powder. Stir until smooth and the ingredients are well blended. 2. Spread the mixture in a baking pan. Top with the pizza sauce, spreading to the edges. Sprinkle with the remaining 56 g shredded cheese. Arrange the pepperoni slices on top of the cheese. Top with the black olives and green onion. 3. Place the pan in the air fryer basket. Set the air fryer to 180ºC for 10 minutes, or until the pepperoni is beginning to brown on the edges and the cheese is bubbly and lightly browned. 4. Let stand for 5 minutes before serving with mixed vegetables, toasted baguette slices, pitta chips, or tortilla chips.

# Roasted Grape Dip

**Prep time: 10 minutes | Cook time: 8 to 12 minutes | Serves 6**

| | |
|---|---|
| 475 g seedless red grapes, rinsed and patted dry | 240 ml low-fat Greek yoghurt |
| 1 tablespoon apple cider vinegar | 2 tablespoons semi-skimmed milk |
| 1 tablespoon honey | 2 tablespoons minced fresh basil |

1. In the air fryer basket, sprinkle the grapes with the cider vinegar and drizzle with the honey. Toss to coat. Roast the grapes at 190ºC for 8 to 12 minutes, or until shrivelled but still soft. Remove from the air fryer. 2. In a medium-sized bowl, stir together the yoghurt and milk. 3. Gently blend in the grapes and basil. Serve immediately or cover and chill for 1 to 2 hours.

## Chilli-brined Fried Calamari

**Prep time: 20 minutes | Cook time: 8 minutes | Serves 2**

| | |
|---|---|
| 1 (227 g) jar sweet or hot pickled cherry peppers | black pepper, to taste |
| 227 g calamari bodies and tentacles, bodies cut into ½-inch-wide rings | 3 large eggs, lightly beaten |
| | Cooking spray |
| | 120 ml mayonnaise |
| 1 lemon | 1 teaspoon finely chopped rosemary |
| 200 g plain flour | 1 garlic clove, minced |
| Rock salt and freshly ground | |

1. Drain the pickled pepper brine into a large bowl and tear the peppers into bite-size strips. Add the pepper strips and calamari to the brine and let stand in the refrigerator for 20 minutes or up to 2 hours. 2. Grate the lemon zest into a large bowl then whisk in the flour and season with salt and pepper. Dip the calamari and pepper strips in the egg, then toss them in the flour mixture until fully coated. Spray the calamari and peppers liberally with cooking spray, then transfer half to the air fryer. Air fry at 200ºC, shaking the basket halfway into cooking, until the calamari is fully cooked and golden, about 8 minutes. Transfer to a plate and repeat with the remaining pieces. 3. In a small bowl, whisk together the mayonnaise, rosemary, and garlic. Squeeze half the zested lemon to get 1 tablespoon of juice and stir it into the sauce. Season with salt and pepper. Cut the remaining zested lemon half into 4 small wedges and serve alongside the calamari, peppers, and sauce.

## Old Bay Chicken Wings

**Prep time: 10 minutes | Cook time: 12 to 15 minutes | Serves 4**

| | |
|---|---|
| 2 tablespoons Old Bay or all-purpose seasoning | 900 g chicken wings, patted dry |
| 2 teaspoons baking powder | Cooking spray |
| 2 teaspoons salt | |

1. Preheat the air fryer to 200ºC. Lightly spray the air fryer basket with cooking spray. 2. Combine the seasoning, baking powder, and salt in a large zip-top plastic bag. Add the chicken wings, seal, and shake until the wings are thoroughly coated in the seasoning mixture. 3. Lay the chicken wings in the air fryer basket in a single layer and lightly mist with cooking spray. You may need to work in batches to avoid overcrowding. 4. Air fry for 12 to 15 minutes, flipping the wings halfway through, or until the wings are lightly browned and the internal temperature reaches at least 74ºC on a meat thermometer. 5. Remove from the basket to a plate and repeat with the remaining chicken wings. 6. Serve hot.

## Ranch Oyster Snack Crackers

**Prep time: 3 minutes | Cook time: 12 minutes | Serves 6**

| | |
|---|---|
| Oil, for spraying | weed |
| 60 ml olive oil | ½ teaspoon garlic powder |
| 2 teaspoons dry ranch dressing mix | ½ teaspoon salt |
| 1 teaspoon chili powder | 1 (255 g) bag water biscuits or low-salt biscuits |
| ½ teaspoon dried fresh dill | |

1. Preheat the air fryer to 160ºC. Line the air fryer basket with baking paper and spray lightly with oil. 2. In a large bowl, mix together the olive oil, ranch dressing mix, chili powder, fresh dill, garlic, and salt. Add the crackers and toss until evenly coated. 3. Place the mixture in the prepared basket. 4. Cook for 10 to 12 minutes, shaking or stirring every 3 to 4 minutes, or until crisp and golden.

## Prawns Toasts with Sesame Seeds

**Prep time: 15 minutes | Cook time: 6 to 8 minutes | Serves 4 to 6**

| | |
|---|---|
| 230 g raw prawns, peeled and deveined | 1 to 2 teaspoons sriracha sauce |
| 1 egg, beaten | 1 teaspoon soy sauce |
| 2 spring onions, chopped, plus more for garnish | ½ teaspoon toasted sesame oil |
| | 6 slices thinly sliced white sandwich bread |
| 2 tablespoons finely chopped fresh coriander | 75 g sesame seeds |
| 2 teaspoons grated fresh ginger | Cooking spray |
| | Thai chilli sauce, for serving |

1. Preheat the air fryer to 200ºC. Spritz the air fryer basket with cooking spray. 2. In a food processor, add the prawns, egg, spring onions, coriander, ginger, sriracha sauce, soy sauce and sesame oil, and pulse until chopped finely. You'll need to stop the food processor occasionally to scrape down the sides. Transfer the prawns mixture to a bowl. 3. On a clean work surface, cut the crusts off the sandwich bread. Using a brush, generously brush one side of each slice of bread with prawns mixture. 4. Place the sesame seeds on a plate. Press bread slices, prawns-side down, into sesame seeds to coat evenly. Cut each slice diagonally into quarters. 5. Spread the coated slices in a single layer in the air fryer basket. 6. Air fry in batches for 6 to 8 minutes, or until golden and crispy. Flip the bread slices halfway through. Repeat with the remaining bread slices. 7. Transfer to a plate and let cool for 5 minutes. Top with the chopped spring onions and serve warm with Thai chilli sauce.

## Taco-Spiced Chickpeas

**Prep time: 5 minutes | Cook time: 17 minutes | Serves 3**

| | |
|---|---|
| Oil, for spraying | ½ teaspoon cumin powder |
| 1 (439 g) can chickpeas, drained | ½ teaspoon salt |
| | ½ teaspoon garlic powder |
| 1 teaspoon chili powder | 2 teaspoons lime juice |

1. Line the air fryer basket with baking paper and spray lightly with oil. Place the chickpeas in the prepared basket. 2. Air fry at 200ºC for 17 minutes, shaking or stirring the chickpeas and spraying lightly with oil every 5 to 7 minutes. 3. In a small bowl, mix together the chili powder, cumin, salt, and garlic. 4. When 2 to 3 minutes of cooking time remain, sprinkle half of the seasoning mix over the chickpeas. Finish cooking. 5. Transfer the chickpeas to a medium-sized bowl and toss with the remaining seasoning mix and the lime juice. Serve immediately.

## Crunchy Basil White Beans

**Prep time: 2 minutes | Cook time: 19 minutes | Serves 2**

| | |
|---|---|
| 1 (425 g) can cooked white beans | chopped |
| 2 tablespoons olive oil | ¼ teaspoon garlic powder |
| 1 teaspoon fresh sage, | ¼ teaspoon salt, divided |
| | 1 teaspoon chopped fresh basil |

1. Preheat the air fryer to 190ºC. 2. In a medium-sized bowl, mix together the beans, olive oil, sage, garlic, ⅛ teaspoon salt, and basil. 3. Pour the white beans into the air fryer and spread them out in a single layer. 4. Bake for 10 minutes. Stir and continue cooking for an additional 5 to 9 minutes, or until they reach your preferred level of crispiness. 5. Toss with the remaining ⅛ teaspoon salt before serving.

## Stuffed Fried Mushrooms

**Prep time: 20 minutes | Cook time: 10 to 11 minutes | Serves 10**

| | |
|---|---|
| 50 g panko breadcrumbs | 1 (227 g) package soft white cheese, at room temperature |
| ½ teaspoon freshly ground black pepper | 20 cremini or button mushrooms, stemmed |
| ½ teaspoon onion powder | |
| ½ teaspoon cayenne pepper | 1 to 2 tablespoons oil |

1. In a medium-sized bowl, whisk the breadcrumbs, black pepper, onion powder, and cayenne until blended. 2. Add the soft white cheese and mix until well blended. Fill each mushroom top with 1 teaspoon of the soft white cheese mixture 3. Preheat the air fryer to 180ºC. Line the air fryer basket with a piece of baking paper paper. 4. Place the mushrooms on the baking paper and spritz with oil. 5. Cook for 5 minutes. Shake the basket and cook for 5 to 6 minutes more until the filling is firm and the mushrooms are soft.

## Root Veggie Chips with Herb Salt

**Prep time: 10 minutes | Cook time: 8 minutes | Serves 2**

| | |
|---|---|
| 1 parsnip, washed | Cooking spray |
| 1 small beetroot, washed | Herb Salt: |
| 1 small turnip, washed | ¼ teaspoon rock salt |
| ½ small sweet potato, washed | 2 teaspoons finely chopped fresh parsley |
| 1 teaspoon olive oil | |

1. Preheat the air fryer to 180ºC. 2. Peel and thinly slice the parsnip, beetroot, turnip, and sweet potato, then place the mixed vegetables in a large bowl, add the olive oil, and toss. 3. Spray the air fryer basket with cooking spray, then place the mixed vegetables in the basket and air fry for 8 minutes, gently shaking the basket halfway through. 4. While the chips cook, make the herb salt in a small bowl by combining the rock salt and parsley. 5. Remove the chips and place on a serving plate, then sprinkle the herb salt on top and allow to cool for 2 to 3 minutes before serving.

## Artichoke and Olive Pitta Flatbread

**Prep time: 5 minutes | Cook time: 10 minutes | Serves 4**

| | |
|---|---|
| 2 wholewheat pitta bread | sliced |
| 2 tablespoons olive oil, divided | 70 g Kalamata olives |
| | 30 g shredded Parmesan |
| 2 garlic cloves, minced | 55 g crumbled feta cheese |
| ¼ teaspoon salt | Chopped fresh parsley, for garnish (optional) |
| 120 g canned artichoke hearts, | |

1. Preheat the air fryer to 190ºC. 2. Brush each pitta with 1 tablespoon olive oil, then sprinkle the minced garlic and salt over the top. 3. Distribute the artichoke hearts, olives, and cheeses evenly between the two pitta bread, and place both into the air fryer to bake for 10 minutes. 4. Remove the pitta bread and cut them into 4 pieces each before serving. Sprinkle parsley over the top, if desired.

## Poutine with Waffle Fries

**Prep time: 10 minutes | Cook time: 15 to 17 minutes | Serves 4**

| | |
|---|---|
| 225 g frozen waffle cut fries | 2 spring onions, sliced |
| 2 teaspoons olive oil | 90 g shredded Swiss cheese |
| 1 red pepper, chopped | 120 ml bottled chicken gravy |

1. Preheat the air fryer to 190°C. 2. Toss the waffle fries with the olive oil and place in the air fryer basket. Air fry for 10 to 12 minutes, or until the fries are crisp and light golden, shaking the basket halfway through the cooking time. 3. Transfer the fries to a baking pan and top with the pepper, spring onions, and cheese. Air fry for 3 minutes, or until the mixed vegetables are crisp and tender. 4. Remove the pan from the air fryer and drizzle the gravy over the fries. Air fry for 2 minutes, or until the gravy is hot. 5. Serve immediately.

## Classic Spring Rolls

**Prep time: 10 minutes | Cook time: 9 minutes | Makes 16 spring rolls**

| | |
|---|---|
| 4 teaspoons toasted sesame oil | 80 g grated carrot |
| 6 medium garlic cloves, minced or pressed | ½ teaspoon sea salt |
| | 16 rice paper wrappers |
| 1 tablespoon grated peeled fresh ginger | Cooking oil spray (sunflower, safflower, or refined coconut) |
| 70 g thinly sliced shiitake mushrooms | Gluten-free sweet and sour sauce or Thai sweet chilli sauce, for serving (optional) |
| 500 g chopped green cabbage | |

1. Place a wok or sauté pan over medium heat until hot. 2. Add the sesame oil, garlic, ginger, mushrooms, cabbage, carrot, and salt. Cook for 3 to 4 minutes, stirring often, until the cabbage is lightly wilted. Remove the pan from the heat. 3. Gently run a rice paper under water. Lay it on a flat non-absorbent surface. Place about 30 g of the cabbage filling in the middle. Once the wrapper is soft enough to roll, fold the bottom up over the filling, fold in the sides, and roll the wrapper all the way up. (Basically, make a tiny burrito.) 4. Repeat step 3 to make the remaining spring rolls until you have the number of spring rolls you want to cook right now (and the amount that will fit in the air fryer basket in a single layer without them touching each other). Refrigerate any leftover filling in an airtight container for about 1 week. 5. Insert the crisper plate into the basket and the basket into the unit. Preheat the unit by selecting AIR FRY, setting the temperature to 200°C, and setting the time to 3 minutes. Select START/STOP to begin. 6. Once the unit is preheated, spray the crisper plate and the basket with cooking oil. Place the spring rolls into the basket, leaving a little room between them so they don't stick to each other. Spray the top of each spring roll with cooking oil. 7. Select AIR FRY, set the temperature to 200°C, and set the time to 9 minutes. Select START/STOP to begin. 8. When the cooking is complete, the egg rolls should be crisp-ish and lightly browned. Serve immediately, plain or with a sauce of choice.

## Mexican Potato Skins

**Prep time: 10 minutes | Cook time: 55 minutes | Serves 6**

| | |
|---|---|
| Olive oil | beans |
| 6 medium russet potatoes or Maris Piper potatoes, scrubbed | 1 tablespoon taco seasoning |
| | 120 g salsa |
| Salt and freshly ground black pepper, to taste | 80 g low-fat shredded Cheddar cheese |
| 260 g fat-free refried black | |

1. Spray the air fryer basket lightly with olive oil. 2. Spray the potatoes lightly with oil and season with salt and pepper. Pierce each potato a few times with a fork. 3. Place the potatoes in the air fryer basket. Air fry at 200°C until fork-tender, 30 to 40 minutes. The cooking time will depend on the size of the potatoes. You can cook the potatoes in the microwave or a standard oven, but they won't get the same lovely crispy skin they will get in the air fryer. 4. While the potatoes are cooking, in a small bowl, mix together the beans and taco seasoning. Set aside until the potatoes are cool enough to handle. 5. Cut each potato in half lengthwise. Scoop out most of the insides, leaving about ¼ inch in the skins so the potato skins hold their shape. 6. Season the insides of the potato skins with salt and black pepper. Lightly spray the insides of the potato skins with oil. You may need to cook them in batches. 7. Place them into the air fryer basket, skin-side down, and air fry until crisp and golden, 8 to 10 minutes. 8. Transfer the skins to a work surface and spoon ½ tablespoon of seasoned refried black beans into each one. Top each with 2 teaspoons salsa and 1 tablespoon shredded Cheddar cheese. 9. Place filled potato skins in the air fryer basket in a single layer. Lightly spray with oil. 10. Air fry until the cheese is melted and bubbly, 2 to 3 minutes.

# Beef and Mango Skewers

**Prep time: 10 minutes | Cook time: 4 to 7 minutes | Serves 4**

| | |
|---|---|
| 340 g beef sirloin tip, cut into 1-inch cubes | ½ teaspoon dried marjoram |
| 2 tablespoons balsamic vinegar | Pinch of salt |
| 1 tablespoon olive oil | Freshly ground black pepper, to taste |
| 1 tablespoon honey | 1 mango |

1. Preheat the air fryer to 200°C. 2. Put the beef cubes in a medium-sized bowl and add the balsamic vinegar, olive oil, honey, marjoram, salt, and pepper. Mix well, then massage the marinade into the beef with your hands. Set aside. 3. To prepare the mango, stand it on end and cut the skin off, using a sharp knife. Then carefully cut around the oval pit to remove the flesh. Cut the mango into 1-inch cubes. 4. Thread metal skewers alternating with three beef cubes and two mango cubes. 5. Roast the skewers in the air fryer basket for 4 to 7 minutes, or until the beef is browned and at least 63°C. 6. Serve hot.

# Chapter 10 Desserts

# Chapter 10 Desserts

## Crustless Peanut Butter Cheesecake

**Prep time: 10 minutes | Cook time: 10 minutes | Serves 2**

| 110 g cream cheese, softened | sugar-added peanut butter |
| 2 tablespoons powdered sweetener | ½ teaspoon vanilla extract |
| 1 tablespoon all-natural, no- | 1 large egg, whisked |

1. In a medium bowl, mix cream cheese and sweetener until smooth. Add peanut butter and vanilla, mixing until smooth. Add egg and stir just until combined. 2. Spoon mixture into an ungreased springform pan and place into air fryer basket. Adjust the temperature to 150°C and bake for 10 minutes. Edges will be firm, but center will be mostly set with only a small amount of jiggle when done. 3. Let pan cool at room temperature 30 minutes, cover with plastic wrap, then place into refrigerator at least 2 hours. Serve chilled.

## Brown Sugar Banana Bread

**Prep time: 20 minutes | Cook time: 22 to 24 minutes | Serves 4**

| 195 g packed light brown sugar | 1½ teaspoons baking powder |
| 1 large egg, beaten | 1 teaspoon ground cinnamon |
| 2 tablespoons unsalted butter, melted | ½ teaspoon salt |
| 120 ml milk, whole or semi-skimmed | 1 banana, mashed |
| 250 g All-purpose flour | 1 to 2 tablespoons coconut, or avocado oil oil |
|  | 20 g icing sugar (optional) |

1. In a large bowl, stir together the brown sugar, egg, melted butter, and milk. 2. In a medium bowl, whisk the flour, baking powder, cinnamon, and salt until blended. Add the flour mixture to the sugar mixture and stir just to blend. 3. Add the mashed banana and stir to combine. 4. Preheat the air fryer to 180°C. Spritz 2 mini loaf pans with oil. 5. Evenly divide the batter between the prepared pans and place them in the air fryer basket. 6. Cook for 22 to 24 minutes, or until a knife inserted into the middle of the loaves comes out clean. 7. Dust the warm loaves with icing sugar (if using).

## Caramelized Fruit Skewers

**Prep time: 10 minutes | Cook time: 3 to 5 minutes | Serves 4**

| 2 peaches, peeled, pitted, and thickly sliced | ½ teaspoon ground cinnamon |
| 3 plums, halved and pitted | ¼ teaspoon ground allspice |
| 3 nectarines, halved and pitted | Pinch cayenne pepper |
| 1 tablespoon honey | Special Equipment: |
|  | 8 metal skewers |

1. Preheat the air fryer to 200°C. 2. Thread, alternating peaches, plums, and nectarines, onto the metal skewers that fit into the air fryer. 3. Thoroughly combine the honey, cinnamon, allspice, and cayenne in a small bowl. Brush the glaze generously over the fruit skewers. 4. Transfer the fruit skewers to the air fryer basket. You may need to cook in batches to avoid overcrowding. 5. Air fry for 3 to 5 minutes, or until the fruit is caramelized. 6. Remove from the basket and repeat with the remaining fruit skewers. 7. Let the fruit skewers rest for 5 minutes before serving.

## Dark Brownies

**Prep time: 10 minutes | Cook time: 11 to 13 minutes | Serves 4**

| 1 egg | 30 g cocoa |
| 85 g granulated sugar | Cooking spray |
| ¼ teaspoon salt | Optional: |
| ½ teaspoon vanilla | Vanilla ice cream |
| 55 g unsalted butter, melted | Caramel sauce |
| 15 g All-purpose flour, plus 2 tablespoons | Whipped cream |

1. Beat together egg, sugar, salt, and vanilla until light. 2. Add melted butter and mix well. 3. Stir in flour and cocoa. 4. Spray a baking pan with raised sides lightly with cooking spray. 5. Spread batter in pan and bake at 160°C for 11 to 13 minutes. Cool and cut into 4 large squares or 16 small brownie bites.

## Indian Toast and Milk

**Prep time: 10 minutes | Cook time: 20 minutes | Serves 4**

| 305 g sweetened, condensed milk | 4 slices white bread |
| --- | --- |
| 240 ml evaporated milk | 2 to 3 tablespoons ghee or butter, softened |
| 240 ml single cream | 2 tablespoons crushed pistachios, for garnish (optional) |
| 1 teaspoon ground cardamom, plus additional for garnish | |
| 1 pinch saffron threads | |

1. In a baking pan, combine the condensed milk, evaporated milk, half-and-half, cardamom, and saffron. Stir until well combined. 2. Place the pan in the air fryer basket. Set the air fryer to 180°C for 15 minutes, stirring halfway through the cooking time. Remove the sweetened milk from the air fryer and set aside. 3. Cut each slice of bread into two triangles. Brush each side with ghee. Place the bread in the air fryer basket. Keeping the air fryer on 180°C cook for 5 minutes or until golden brown and toasty. 4. Remove the bread from the air fryer. Arrange two triangles in each of four wide, shallow bowls. Pour the hot milk mixture on top of the bread and let soak for 30 minutes. 5. Garnish with pistachios if using, and sprinkle with additional cardamom.

## Apple Fries

**Prep time: 10 minutes | Cook time: 7 minutes | Serves 8**

| Coconut, or avocado oil, for spraying | 40 g granulated sugar |
| --- | --- |
| 55 g All-purpose flour | 1 teaspoon ground cinnamon |
| 3 large eggs, beaten | 3 large Gala apples, peeled, cored and cut into wedges |
| 100 g crushed digestive biscuits | 240 ml caramel sauce, warmed |

1. Preheat the air fryer to 190°C. Line the air fryer basket with baking paper and spray lightly with oil. 2. Place the flour and beaten eggs in separate bowls and set aside. In another bowl, mix together the crushed biscuits, sugar and cinnamon. 3. Working one at a time, coat the apple wedges in the flour, dip in the egg and then dredge in the biscuit mix until evenly coated. 4. Place the apples in the prepared basket, taking care not to overlap, and spray lightly with oil. You may need to work in batches, depending on the size of your air fryer. 5. Cook for 5 minutes, flip, spray with oil, and cook for another 2 minutes, or until crunchy and golden brown. 6. Drizzle the caramel sauce over the top and serve.

## Butter Flax Cookies

**Prep time: 25 minutes | Cook time: 20 minutes | Serves 4**

| 115 g almond meal | A pinch of coarse salt |
| --- | --- |
| 2 tablespoons flaxseed meal | 1 large egg, room temperature. |
| 30 g monk fruit, or equivalent sweetener | 110 g unsalted butter, room temperature |
| 1 teaspoon baking powder | 1 teaspoon vanilla extract |
| A pinch of grated nutmeg | |

1. Mix the almond meal, flaxseed meal, monk fruit, baking powder, grated nutmeg, and salt in a bowl. 2. In a separate bowl, whisk the egg, butter, and vanilla extract. 3. Stir the egg mixture into dry mixture; mix to combine well or until it forms a nice, soft dough. 4. Roll your dough out and cut out with a cookie cutter of your choice. Bake in the preheated air fryer at 180°C for 10 minutes. Decrease the temperature to 160°C and cook for 10 minutes longer. Bon appétit!

## Pineapple Wontons

**Prep time: 15 minutes | Cook time: 15 to 18 minutes per batch | Serves 5**

| 225 g cream cheese | 20 wonton wrappers |
| --- | --- |
| 170 g finely chopped fresh pineapple | Cooking oil spray |

1. In a small microwave-safe bowl, heat the cream cheese in the microwave on high power for 20 seconds to soften. 2. In a medium bowl, stir together the cream cheese and pineapple until mixed well. 3. Lay out the wonton wrappers on a work surface. A clean table or large cutting board works well. 4. Spoon 1½ teaspoons of the cream cheese mixture onto each wrapper. Be careful not to overfill. 5. Fold each wrapper diagonally across to form a triangle. Bring the 2 bottom corners up toward each other. Do not close the wrapper yet. Bring up the 2 open sides and push out any air. Squeeze the open edges together to seal. 6. Insert the crisper plate into the basket and the basket into the unit. Preheat the air fryer to 200°C. 7. Once the unit is preheated, spray the crisper plate with cooking oil. Place the wontons into the basket. You can work in batches or stack the wontons. Spray the wontons with the cooking oil. 8. Cook wontons for 10 minutes, then remove the basket, flip each wonton, and spray them with more oil. Reinsert the basket to resume cooking for 5 to 8 minutes more until the wontons are light golden brown and crisp. 9. If cooking in batches, remove the cooked wontons from the basket and repeat steps 7 and 8 for the remaining wontons. 10. When the cooking is complete, cool for 5 minutes before serving.

## Grilled Pineapple Dessert

**Prep time: 5 minutes | Cook time: 12 minutes | Serves 4**

| | |
|---|---|
| Coconut, or avocado oil for misting, or cooking spray | juice |
| 4½-inch-thick slices fresh pineapple, core removed | 2 tablespoons slivered almonds, toasted |
| 1 tablespoon honey | Vanilla frozen yogurt, coconut sorbet, or ice cream |
| ¼ teaspoon brandy, or apple | |

1. Spray both sides of pineapple slices with oil or cooking spray. Place into air fryer basket. 2. Air fry at 200°C for 6 minutes. Turn slices over and cook for an additional 6 minutes. 3. Mix together the honey and brandy. 4. Remove cooked pineapple slices from air fryer, sprinkle with toasted almonds, and drizzle with honey mixture. 5. Serve with a scoop of frozen yogurt or sorbet on the side.

## Zucchini Bread

**Prep time: 10 minutes | Cook time: 40 minutes | Serves 12**

| | |
|---|---|
| 220 g coconut flour | 1 teaspoon vanilla extract |
| 2 teaspoons baking powder | 3 eggs, beaten |
| 150 g granulated sweetener | 1 courgette, grated |
| 120 ml coconut oil, melted | 1 teaspoon ground cinnamon |
| 1 teaspoon apple cider vinegar | |

1. In the mixing bowl, mix coconut flour with baking powder, sweetener, coconut oil, apple cider vinegar, vanilla extract, eggs, courgette, and ground cinnamon. 2. Transfer the mixture into the air fryer basket and flatten it in the shape of the bread. 3. Cook the bread at 180°C for 40 minutes.

## Lime Bars

**Prep time: 10 minutes | Cook time: 33 minutes | Makes 12 bars**

| | |
|---|---|
| 140 g blanched finely ground almond flour, divided | 4 tablespoons salted butter, melted |
| 40 g powdered sweetener, divided | 120 ml fresh lime juice |
| | 2 large eggs, whisked |

1. In a medium bowl, mix together 110 g flour, 25 g sweetener, and butter. Press mixture into bottom of an ungreased round nonstick cake pan. 2. Place pan into air fryer basket. Adjust the temperature to 150°C and bake for 13 minutes. Crust will be brown and set in the middle when done. 3. Allow to cool in pan 10 minutes. 4. In a medium bowl, combine remaining flour, remaining sweetener, lime juice, and eggs. Pour mixture over cooled crust and return to air fryer for 20 minutes. Top will be browned and firm when done. 5. Let cool completely in pan, about 30 minutes, then chill covered in the refrigerator 1 hour. Serve chilled.

## Boston Cream Donut Holes

**Prep time: 30 minutes | Cook time: 4 minutes per batch | Makes 24 donut holes**

| | |
|---|---|
| 100 g bread flour | Vegetable oil |
| 1 teaspoon active dry yeast | Custard Filling: |
| 1 tablespoon granulated sugar | 95 g box French vanilla instant pudding mix |
| ¼ teaspoon salt | 175 ml whole milk |
| 120 ml warm milk | 60 ml heavy cream |
| ½ teaspoon pure vanilla extract | Chocolate Glaze: |
| 2 egg yolks | 170 g chocolate chips |
| 2 tablespoons unsalted butter, melted | 80 ml heavy cream |

1. Combine the flour, yeast, sugar, and salt in the bowl of a stand mixer. Add the milk, vanilla, egg yolks and butter. Mix until the dough starts to come together in a ball. Transfer the dough to a floured surface and knead the dough by hand for 2 minutes. Shape the dough into a ball, place it in a large, oiled bowl, cover the bowl with a clean kitchen towel and let the dough rise for 1 to 1½ hours or until the dough has doubled in size. 2. When the dough has risen, punch it down and roll it into a 24-inch log. Cut the dough into 24 pieces and roll each piece into a ball. Place the dough balls on a baking sheet and let them rise for another 30 minutes. 3. Preheat the air fryer to 200°C. 4. Spray or brush the dough balls lightly with vegetable oil and air fry eight at a time for 4 minutes, turning them over halfway through the cooking time. 5. While donut holes are cooking, make the filling and chocolate glaze. Make the filling: Use an electric hand mixer to beat the French vanilla pudding, milk and ¼ cup of heavy cream together for 2 minutes. 6. Make the chocolate glaze: Place the chocolate chips in a medium-sized bowl. Bring the heavy cream to a boil on the stovetop and pour it over the chocolate chips. Stir until the chips are melted and the glaze is smooth. 7. To fill the donut holes, place the custard filling in a pastry bag with a long tip. Poke a hole into the side of the donut hole with a small knife. Wiggle the knife around to make room for the filling. Place the pastry bag tip into the hole and slowly squeeze the custard into the center of the donut. Dip the top half of the donut into the chocolate glaze, letting any excess glaze drip back into the bowl. Let the glazed donut holes sit for a few minutes before serving.

# Blueberry Cream Cheese Bread Pudding

**Prep time: 15 minutes | Cook time: 1 hour 10 minutes | Serves 6**

| | |
|---|---|
| 240 ml single cream | 4 to 5 croissants, cubed |
| 4 large eggs | 150 g blueberries |
| 50 g granulated sugar, plus 3 tablespoons | 110 g cream cheese, cut into small cubes |
| 1 teaspoon pure lemon extract | |

1. In a large bowl, combine the cream, eggs, 65 g of sugar, and the extract. Whisk until well combined. Add the cubed croissants, blueberries, and cream cheese. Toss gently until everything is thoroughly combined; set aside. 2. Place a 3-cup Bundt pan (a tube or Angel Food cake pan would work too) in the air fryer basket. Preheat the air fryer to 200°C. 3. Sprinkle the remaining 3 tablespoons sugar in the bottom of the hot pan. Cook for 10 minutes, or until the sugar caramelizes. Tip the pan to spread the caramel evenly across the bottom of the pan. 4. Remove the pan from the air fryer and pour in the bread mixture, distributing it evenly across the pan. Place the pan in the air fryer basket. Set the air fryer to 180°C and bake for 60 minutes, or until the custard is set in the middle. Let stand for 10 minutes before unmolding onto a serving plate.

# Lemon Poppy Seed Macaroons

**Prep time: 10 minutes | Cook time: 14 minutes | Makes 1 dozen**

| | |
|---|---|
| cookies | 1 teaspoon lemon extract |
| 2 large egg whites, room temperature | ¼ teaspoon fine sea salt |
| 20 g powdered sweetener | 190 g desiccated unsweetened coconut |
| 2 tablespoons grated lemon zest, plus more for garnish if desired | Lemon Icing: |
| | 25 g sweetener |
| 2 teaspoons poppy seeds | 1 tablespoon lemon juice |

1. Preheat the air fryer to 160°C. Line a pie pan or a casserole dish that will fit inside your air fryer with baking paper. 2. Place the egg whites in a medium-sized bowl and use a hand mixer on high to beat the whites until stiff peaks form. Add the sweetener, lemon zest, poppy seeds, lemon extract, and salt. Mix on low until combined. Gently fold in the coconut with a rubber spatula. 3. Use a 1-inch cookie scoop to place the cookies on the baking paper, spacing them about ¼ inch apart. Place the pan in the air fryer and bake for 12 to 14 minutes, until the cookies are golden, and a toothpick inserted into the center comes out clean. 4. While the cookies bake, make the lemon icing: Place the sweetener in a small bowl. Add the lemon juice and stir well. If the icing is too thin, add a little more sweetener. If the icing is too thick, add a little more lemon juice. 5. Remove the cookies from the air fryer and allow to cool for about 10 minutes, then drizzle with the icing. Garnish with lemon zest, if desired. Store leftovers in an airtight container in the fridge for up to 5 days or in the freezer for up to a month.

# Chocolate Soufflés

**Prep time: 5 minutes | Cook time: 14 minutes | Serves 2**

| | |
|---|---|
| Butter and sugar for greasing the ramekins | sugar |
| 85 g semi-sweet chocolate, chopped | ½ teaspoon pure vanilla extract |
| 55 g unsalted butter | 2 tablespoons All-purpose flour |
| 2 eggs, yolks and white separated | Icing sugar, for dusting the finished soufflés |
| 3 tablespoons granulated | Heavy cream, for serving |

1. Butter and sugar two 6-ounce (170 g) ramekins. (Butter the ramekins and then coat the butter with sugar by shaking it around in the ramekin and dumping out any excess.) 2. Melt the chocolate and butter together, either in the microwave or in a double boiler. In a separate bowl, beat the egg yolks vigorously. Add the sugar and the vanilla extract and beat well again. Drizzle in the chocolate and butter, mixing well. Stir in the flour, combining until there are no lumps. 3. Preheat the air fryer to 160°C. 4. In a separate bowl, whisk the egg whites to soft peak stage (the point at which the whites can almost stand up on the end of your whisk). Fold the whipped egg whites into the chocolate mixture gently and in stages. 5. Transfer the batter carefully to the buttered ramekins, leaving about ½-inch at the top. (You may have a little extra batter, depending on how airy the batter is, so you might be able to squeeze out a third soufflé if you want to.) Place the ramekins into the air fryer basket and air fry for 14 minutes. The soufflés should have risen nicely and be brown on top. (Don't worry if the top gets a little dark, you'll be covering it with icing sugar in the next step.) 6. Dust with icing sugar and serve immediately with heavy cream to pour over the top at the table.

Printed in Great Britain
by Amazon